Watercharms

OCEAN-REIKI MEDITATIONS

Sylvia M. DeSantis, M.A., R.M.T.

Schiffer Publishing Ltd.

4880 Lower Valley Road, Atglen, Pennsylvania 19310

Text by author
Photos by Dax J. Finley

Library of Congress Control Number: 2011938692

Designed by Justin Watkinson Cover by Bruce Waters
Type set in Book Antiqua/Helvetica Neue Pro/Shelly Allegro BT

ISBN: 978-0-7643-3914-1
Printed in China

Schiffer Books are available at special discounts for bulk purchases for sales promotions or premiums. Special editions, including personalized covers, corporate imprints, and excerpts can be created in large quantities for special needs.

For more information contact the publisher:

Published by Schiffer Publishing Ltd.
4880 Lower Valley Road
Atglen, PA 19310
Phone: (610) 593-1777; Fax: (610) 593-2002
E-mail: Info@schifferbooks.com

For the largest selection of fine reference books on this and related subjects, please visit our website at
www.schifferbooks.com
We are always looking for people to write books on new and related subjects. If you have an idea for a book, please contact us at
proposals@schifferbooks.com

This book may be purchased from the publisher.
Include $5.00 for shipping.
Please try your bookstore first.
You may write for a free catalog.

In Europe, Schiffer books are distributed by
Bushwood Books
6 Marksbury Ave.
Kew Gardens
Surrey TW9 4JF England
Phone: 44 (0) 20 8392 8585; Fax: 44 (0) 20 8392 9876
E-mail: info@bushwoodbooks.co.uk
Website: www.bushwoodbooks.co.uk

We must be willing to get rid of the life we've planned, so as to have the life that is waiting for us.

~ Joseph Campbell

It is up to each of us to get very still and say, "This is who I am." No one else defines your life. Only you do.

~ Oprah Winfrey

Don't turn your head away from the signs offered by the sea.

~ Rumi

Acknowlegements

Let me begin with huge thanks to Dinah Roseberry at Schiffer Publishing; she has been an amazing advocate for which I am grateful and delighted. She believed in this book from the beginning and only ever wanted to send it into the light of day. My heartfelt thanks also goes out to three phenomenal healers whose instruction, guidance, and patience has aided me both in life and, in many subtle and profound ways, in producing this work: Deb Klein, of Nittany Health Centre, for introducing me to the Reiki road and showing me how to step upon it; Christine DeHart, for her heartfelt energy and quiet guidance; and most especially Dr. Danielle Beauvais, for her tireless patience, gentle compassion, and genuine wisdom.

Special thanks to the Nawnes: Big and Little. Though far from me in other times and spaces, you're both eternally in my heart. Thanks to Affinity, for the specialness that is you. I must also thank Sandalphon, and PowerStar, along with the many guides, saints, and angels who watch over me; thank you for lifting me on those days when life feels heavy.

I am blessed to have an amazing support network of loving friends and family; thank you to those who came to book signings and supported me so generously. Special thanks to "Bad Aunt Nancy" Benscoter who has supported me tirelessly on this roller coaster ride, no matter how steep or fast; I am blessed to know you. And thanks to all of my dedicated holistic health clients and Reiki students, most especially friend and colleague Stacy Saar; you are a shining star whose dedication makes teaching easy. Thanks as well to Hope Clark at Funds For Writers for her tireless motivation, and for always taking the time to answer my emails, and to Dana Douglas of Dragonfly Therapeutic Massage and Day Spa for her support!

And thanks to my family, close and extended, for their support, especially my brother and attorney, Glenn ("Reiki-ology" indeed, wiseacre) and my mama, Maria, for standing by me. I love you both.

I also would like to thank my dad — may all that pain heal someday.

And, finally, special thanks to my amazing teachers, Nommie, Züs, and Kashmirz, who each day teach me the wonders of unconditional love. And, of course, my partner and gifted photographer, Dax J. Finley. Thank you for everything: keeping Tiny Kitteh busy, making snack runs, fixing my technology, but mostly for your selflessness and patience. I couldn't do all this without your support.

Look what I made for you...

for *Denise*
(1954 – 1981)

Contents

THE 5 *Reiki* PRINCIPLES

by Dr. Mikao Usui

Just for today,
I will not be angry.

Just for today,
I will not worry.

Just for today,
I will be grateful.

Just for today,
I will do my work honestly.

Just for today,
I will be kind to every living thing.

I love being "down the shore." For most people from the Philadelphia area, this quaint colloquialism means one of the many shore points of southern New Jersey. For me, it also refers to the calmest, most perfect place in my heart. The slick jetties and delicious breezes leave me in complete peace. My soul comes home at the ocean. My sister taught this to me.

Suffering from the abusive fallout of my father's war-induced (and untreated) Post-Traumatic Stress Disorder (PTSD), I grew up inside a bubble of fear, a place where undefined terror hummed at the edges of my days, haunting my childhood in subtle and complicated ways. This creeping pain first became apparent in Kindergarten when I was unable to eat or leave the house without panic. This baffled my mother but never stopped my sister from taking me on frequent daytrips to pre-casino Atlantic City, a habit we continued for almost nine years. Denise—thirteen years my senior and my savior—refused to let me hide in my room, instead installing me in the car with sunblock, snacks, and a towel while ignoring my complaints of a stomach ache. With a sister's intuition, she knew exactly what I needed when no one else did.

At first terrified of the too-hot sand, of the water, of drowning, of everything, I eventually learned through her slow and steady patience that waves, in all their power and fury, also wash us free of pain when we most need it. I honestly hadn't known, until she helped me stand in the pounding surf one courageous day, that waves could do more than crush.

Icy popsicles in the sandy heat, teensy sand crabs scuttling underfoot, little tidal pools where bits of seaweed and shell collide… They all worked a magic on me. I began to listen as the ocean talked without screaming, touched without bruising, wrapped me in itself, and wanted nothing in return. I fell deeply, thoroughly, and completely in love.

Because even the smallest glimpse of wholeness strikes us so deeply, we respond intuitively at these times, even if we're just confused children. Our innate healing ability, hand-in-hand with intuition, takes charge and pushes us forward on our journey through old hurts whose suffering we no longer need.

A similarly phenomenal healing power lies within you; perhaps you've noticed it blossom in times of crisis, wondering afterwards where you found the strength. May you have the courage and the desire to acknowledge your perception and open those doorways. This collection of experiences, exercises, and meditations reflects the immediate and unconditional love and compassion available to you right at this moment in your journey towards clearing, clarity, and healing.

9

Step with me into THE gentle TIDE of ocean centered Reiki.

Introduction

Those who love the ocean can rarely articulate exactly why they feel so drawn to one of the most strong and powerful forces on earth. Pretty, calm, rhythmic…no matter how we try to describe its presence, our words fall short. Similarly, we teach our children to daydream of the ocean, peppering them with stories of silly pirates and beautiful sirens. *Watercharms* moves us from myth to reality, fully embracing the ocean's limitless energies to unlock the treasure chest of healing power that lies within each of us.

We already intuitively know how to live life closer to our personal best, even if we don't consciously recognize this or know how to get from here to there. Sometimes, all we know is how we feel— full of fear, stunted with shame, driven by anxiety, dulled by life. When we forget our personal Truths and live from the ego instead, making decisions from a place of pain, shame, and regret, we forget that *living a higher vibrational life path can be ours.*

How to uses this book

Reiki, rediscovered in Japan in the early 1900s and sometimes called "God Consciousness," is a Universal Life Force, or ki, that flows through our bodies and is usually channeled through the hands. In order to offer Reiki, practitioners participate in three to five levels of training, receiving attunements from Reiki Master-Teachers that "turn on" and tap into the energetic flow of energy so often snuffed out during our growth into logical, reasonable adults.

In this book, you will encounter the ocean and its many elements as metaphors for movement, surrender, and focus as a guide on your path to healing. While you will not become a formal Reiki practitioner from reading this book, you will use your imagination and intent to access and understand Reiki's healing potential. If you would like to learn Reiki in order to practice more fully and completely on yourself and others, search massagetherapy.com, a reliable branch of Associated Bodywork and Massage Professionals (ABMP), at http://www.massagetherapy.com/find/ for Master-Teachers in your area.

I guide you in many self-reflective approaches throughout the following chapters and often ask you to journal, sit with your feelings (even when they may be uncomfortable), repeat affirmations and, most especially, be kind to yourself by leaving judgment behind. You might consider recording the healing meditations and affirmations from your favorite chapters in order to listen to them while relaxed. It might also be convenient to dedicate one specific notebook or journal as the place where you keep all of your meditational explorations, exercises, and thoughts. However, you choose to use this book, move at your own pace and enjoy your discovery.

Magical Touch

When we use our hands during Reiki, we experience a form of healing that channels the highest and purest energy already running through our bodies in a way that completely bypasses our minds. Reiki practitioners do this intuitively, placing their hands on those areas to which they are drawn. Consider the similarities between Reiki healing that uses simple touch and a mother showing love and comfort by stroking her sick child's head or friends sharing a huge, heartfelt hug. Touch is magical! When we lovingly touch another being, we transmit not only higher vibrations from the energy fields that surround us, but also love and compassion.

The seven chakras are major, active energy points in our bodies, beginning at the base of the spine and ending at the top of our heads. Each chakra relates to an endocrine gland, corresponds to certain emotions, and is represented by certain colors. As the mind attaches emotion to experience, the brain sends out corresponding chemicals enacting processes that create illness when chakras become blocked or out of sync. My mother, a breast cancer survivor, believes her illness grew from unspoken grief, frustration, and rage at her marriage and turbulent divorce. Reiki helps to shift illness-causing blocks like these, bringing us closer to more balanced states of being.

Reiki's use in partnership with traditional medicine has shown phenomenal results; Reiki can increase the healing effects of other treatments, reduce side effects of medication, increase relaxation, reduce stress, and speed up recovery time. Reiki has even been adopted in operating rooms and post-op/recovery as another way to help patients' bodies heal more quickly from the trauma of invasive procedure.

If this all seems remarkable, you are not alone in thinking this way. When I began working with Reiki, my logical, academic mind ruled every facet of my waking world as I tallied mental to-do lists, worried over bills, and fretted about my life. Simply, I felt unworthy of Reiki because it seemed closer to a Universe I didn't understand and felt completely beyond my capabilities.

Eventually, as a series of life events forced me to see that I needed to release control and accept a stronger, clearer, and healthier life, my intuition blossomed and guided me back to Reiki, into a clearer self-understanding that resulted in a more balanced life. The same can happen to you.

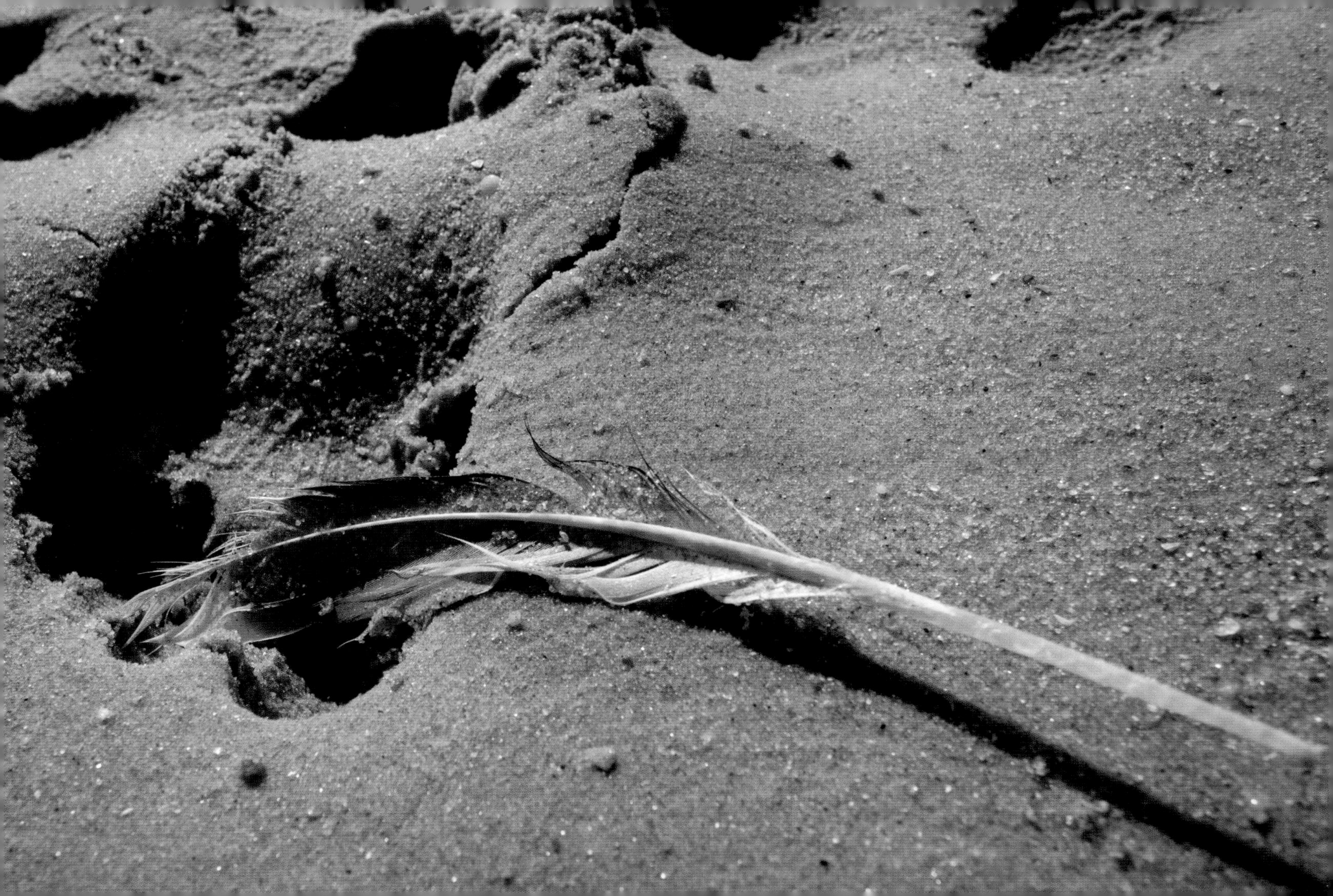

Reiki & Religion

I have encountered resistance to Reiki from those with strong religious beliefs and, to those individuals, I recommend prayer and meditation in order to choose what feels appropriate. Originally raised Catholic, I retain many beliefs, especially those concerning the saints and angels, but I have long since left behind the concept of an angry or punishing God who only praises and rewards those of one particular faith. That holds no resonance for me. How can all spiritual paths except one be wrong? And how could using light and love based on the highest intent for the greatest good be bad? Although they sometimes masquerade as problems or challenges, blessings, hope, and beauty surround each of us every day, no matter our belief system, and inspire us to achieve our personal best. In the end, follow your heart and choose that towards which your intuition guides you.

Alternative Healing Tools

A wonderful way to expand and enhance Reiki's power includes using natural tools and borrowed approaches from other healing modalities and even various religions. These include shell and crystal healing, smudging (cleansing a room with smoke), drumming, repeating affirmations, practicing meditation, listening to soothing music, and journaling.

Any supplemental tool you choose for self-healing should feel good but, like a deep massage or cleansing facial that might initially leave us sore or with a breakout, sometimes we need to draw out impurities and release lower energies before we feel better. For example, journaling and self-exploration can sometimes feel dense and sticky, especially when we uncover information about ourselves we've avoided for a long time; this does not necessarily mean journaling is bad or wrong. Discomfort doesn't always equal a problem.

I often use essential oils, flower essences, candles, crystals, and sometimes even my drum during energy work. Other times I may prop up inspirational cards where I can see them, burn incense, or practice deep breathing. Always choose materials and those tools which speak to your heart, as these will provide the most joy. Learn more about alternative healing tools in the Resources section where I share my favorite and most inspiring book titles and websites.

Give yourself permission to relax and enjoy the meditations and exercises in this text. One need not be religious, yogic, psychic, or especially meditative to enjoy and benefit from the blessings of Reiki healing. With practice, you too can enjoy a healthier self-image, stronger intuition, and clarity in heart, mind, and soul. You hold the power to heal yourself right at this moment.

Let's
begin

Denying *Fear*

Though Conchs look like a common, plain shell, held closely one notices layers of history and complexity within their whirls. Humans have become adept at resisting deep and complex study of ourselves and those around us. We avoid the layers and instead subsist on the obvious and superficial. This reluctance to see deeply and recognize our power strips our strength and confidence in healing ourselves. Facing fear requires desire, commitment, and courage. No wonder we almost always prefer stability to the unknown, choosing familiarity even when other choices would benefit us more completely. By ignoring fear, we cement into place static patterns that affect our lives on every level. Consider… What precious gifts might we unlock once we deny fear's power by embracing and facing it?

The sun scorches my shoulders as I step onto sand so hot I swear the soles of my feet sizzle. I look out across the vast expanse and breathe. Atlantic City's sharp, salty tang meets my nose long before I get near the water's edge. My sister flip-flops forward, her beautiful black hair unspiraling from its loose bun in the stiff, hot breeze. Denise stops, first laying down a towel for me, then herself. She prods me with a sticky finger covered in sun block as I sulk in the scorching glare, sweating unbearably in my beach cover-up.

"Why don't you take that off?"

When I silently pull it tighter she shrugs and lies back, her glossy black hair making a beautiful fan around her face. Mom says she struggled with her weight as a kid, but old pictures don't indicate anything other than a beautiful child with springy black ringlets. She's gorgeous now. Not skinny, but built just right, with full hips and breasts, a curtain of midnight black hair, and an hourglass waist. In my eyes, she's perfect. And I'm fat.

I hear it enough, even from "nice" Catholic kids...kids who sit in chapel with me every morning and smile at the Sisters each afternoon while waiting for their buses. These same kids pick me last, ignore me, and let me know in their own not-so-subtle ways that I'm a piggy, a fat kid.

I yearn to take off my cover-up. The sweat pours down my face, stinging my eyes. My new suit feels itchy and hot although I liked it well enough in the store. My mother bought it thinking that maybe something pretty would pull me from my despair. I'm young but bruised and, while unable to language it, know inherently that I need more than something pretty to fix my wrongs.

I feel a rush of terror and awe at the ferocious ocean pounding a few feet ahead. Waves roar at me and pummel the shoreline, causing fresh, bright stings of spray to reach us on our towels. I am horrified. The pounding waves are too big, too fast, and too loud. They want to devour me, drown me, toss me away

where I will disappear. I clamp my eyes shut and squeeze away the tears, not wanting my sister to see, knowing I won't be able to explain.

Why do we so easily and readily feel devoured by senseless fears? For many of us, the answer lies in trauma. Those who have lived through trauma tend to pull from learned behaviors, letting past horrors map courses that, though highly unlikely, seem very real. In our weakest and most vulnerable moments, although we intellectually recognize our flawed thinking, we still find ourselves paralyzed, immobile, and overwhelmed by a roaring ocean that, from a clearer and less traumatized perspective, is actually just a trickle of water over the toes. At these moments, any little nudge out of paralysis towards a balanced perspective would really benefit us.

My father served in the Korean War many years ago, a war long forgotten and out of style, whose impact left my mother and me scrambling to understand and interpret the overwhelming roar that fear created inside his unsuspecting mind. I remember his boiling, irrational hatred very clearly. First he would get mad with a funny gray flattening of his eyes, and then he would scream at my mother and me in a way that could only be something learned in combat. His voice would boom, and I would quake.

My mother made excuses, explaining that he had come back from war slightly damaged; as a child, this made no sense to me. Why was he still fighting a war two decades old, except now with his family? I spent years secretly believing my father was simply mean and insane.

My mother would tell stories of his post-war behavior—obvious signposts of raging PTSD—during the early years of their marriage, how he would hide under the bed in terror, coming out only after her pleading. She shared how my father had learned to shoot at anyone on the ground, too often killing a man pretending to be dead. According to my mother, my father relived this horror again and again. Then one day he stopped his sad displays, stuffing this horror into a place just below the surface of his consciousness. This sadness and betrayal ultimately took on a cloak of fury. And almost anything could dislodge it.

One night I wake to a high and loud sound, like a baby animal being killed. It takes me a few seconds to understand that the screams come from my mother. She is screaming in terror. I'm paralyzed in my bed, so scared I pee myself. The crack of breaking furniture and shattering glass rattle the house, but then I hear footsteps beating a steady rhythm up the steps, the third step creaking high and loud, the top step groaning under the weight of a footfall. In that moment, I feel insanely scared.

This is it, I think to myself.
I am going to die.

But no, my mother comes to the doorway instead, pale and shaking. Scratching at the light switch with one hand, clutching a laundry basket with the other. The light spreads a watery stain across the room. Her face blossoms with fear, an angry red welt across her papery cheek. It's the middle of the night and the whole world feels dead.

"Mommy…" I whisper, but my father is in the doorway behind her with his crazy eyes. When he finally notices me shaking in my bed, he becomes quiet and curious, like someone fiddling with a crossword

he can't quite figure out, asking me why I'm upset, wondering why I'm not asleep. I feel the wet sheet beneath me, feel my muscles ache from the shaking that won't stop, and am stunned into silence; I have never been so confused.

Guided by my father's pain, I spend much of my childhood damaged but intact, like a snapped shoelace tied and retied at its breaking point until the repair becomes slippery with use, unable to hold together any longer. As a young adult, I jump at loud noises and finally realize how deeply my father's tirades have marked me. When I get upset, I revert to a terrified, impotent state in which I am a small child, shaking uncontrollably and twisted in her sheets, believing she is going to die. The fear, tangible in its power, had developed a life of its own; it had grown into a familiar habit.[1] I grow up leaning towards the pessimistic, allowing myself to feel fleeting relief only when life challenges don't end in complete disaster, becoming horrifically suspicious when things go well of their own accord.

I convince myself that this kind of hypervigilance insures me against the brutality of reality, that the enormous amount of energy it demands is fair exchange for the absurd belief that I'll be prepared to face the next trauma. This delusion frames my entire belief system.

Sardonic life coach Martha Beck reminds us in Finding Your Own North Star that by facing fear, we taste the bittersweet because we grow up. In these moments of clarity, we lose dependency on those we believe keep us safe because we realize that at no age are we ever truly without fear. What a remarkable realization—to finally know that even in adulthood, the pain of fear will shift and twist, but never truly leave because fear is a natural experience for all of us. This allows us to more easily recognize fear cloaked in shadow behaviors that actually look like something else: the ugly behaviors of a bully, the snobbiness of an acquaintance, even the insane anger of a war-damaged veteran. Without our ability to recognize fear, we wouldn't know what it looks like to be brave.2 And only by consciously recognizing the illusory and transitory nature of our fears will we ever move past them. On that fateful day as I stand by the ocean's edge in my itchy suit, the furious ocean embodies for me every fear I have ever owned.

I'm nearly rocked by a wave that gets too close. I've let down my guard and gravitated towards the water, almost swept in during my dangerous daydreaming. I watch Denise hop into the water and gasp when the chilly white foam breaks at her waist. I wonder about that… It's hard to imagine breaking waves when I only ever get my toes wet. I take another step forward, self-consciously sucking in my stomach. I'm so fat starts the same tired voice in my head, but as cool fingers of water wash over my toes, I look out to sea.

The light shimmers, nudging something inside me. I'm exhausted, much too tired for my young body. When does it end? Maybe the fear will eat me alive—it certainly feels that way—but I'm done fighting. I feel a shift and catch my breath, shut down, and step forward. I move towards Denise.

"You're coming in?" I nod and grab her hand, stiffening as a wave bumps by. I'm shaking but she holds on, pulling me up onto her hip the way she'd carry a baby. The gesture—more than I can emotionally bear, everything I desperately need—startles me.

"See, you're okay…" Salty spray washes away her words, leaving us drenched. I hug her neck as she laughs and plunges forward, foam flying up around us. Gulls scream overhead as the bright sun, crisp water, and Denise's love work alchemic magic on me: I transform, right there, into a girl I no longer know.

Stunning myself with my own bravery, I slide from her hip, brace myself and laugh as a wave pushes at me. Stumbling but standing, I forget a school year full of "Fatso," forget to be terrified of the water for the moment, and forget to hate myself as the ocean washes me clean. As the water eddies around my thighs, I feel sorry for my dad, unable to imagine him enjoying a simple pleasure like sitting on the sand or eating a popsicle. I feel acutely aware of where my skin attaches to my bones, of how when I breathe I'm the one pushing the breath in and out.

The physicality of it all, of being pushed around in the ferocious ocean but managing to stand and not drown or otherwise disappear into nothing, stuns me, as though I've literally slipped out of my tired skin and into someone else's. The moment shines like a bright snapshot: I turn my face to the sun and brace for the next wave as my sister rocks with the tide, her smiling face looking back at me.

By knocking down the wall we build from self-loathing and allowing ourselves compassion as we face that roaring wave, we gain the ability to look into the face of that which inspires terror and fear; this is vitally important because in doing so, we arm ourselves with the understanding that we can change our fear habit. What an amazing realization that we hold more than just trauma in our psyche; we hold power! The more we refuse to back down from the fear, the better the opportunity to grow.3 When we touch courage so palpably by refusing to heed the voice that tells us to run run run without reason, we allow ourselves to come to a place of

peace. Shaman Lynn Andrews tells us that to step into fear fully we must recognize it as a self-imposed limit our minds have convinced us are fact4; our self-doubt, while it feels real enough, is part of a story we have created.

And stories can be rewritten.

Neither good nor bad, fear is a lot like pain in the way it takes stock and indicates symptoms — all tremendously useful, within limits. Our relationship to fear becomes troubled when it stops us from growing or moving forward. The key lies in understanding its power rather than denying its existence, an evolved perspective available to us through "whole-spectrum communication," 5 a form of listening to oneself in which one's whole being opens up in a way that allows us to sense and feel information intuitively.

Facing fear and denying its hold on us — really giving it a good hearty listen — involves more than just bravery and determination; this kind of event is a whole-body affair. "Whole-spectrum communication" requires the cooperation of our physical body or "middle self," our spiritual self, and our psychic self

as well. Without all three working in tandem, we can't fully investigate our fear. We've all experienced "whole-spectrum communication" at some time, even if we didn't have the language to name it. When we practice Reiki and become a conduit for healing energy, we necessarily rely upon a whole-spectrum approach as we let go of controlling behaviors and expectations to just "be" in the moment.

I never intended to step into the ocean. The idea of splashing around in the waves had always been reserved for someone else, someone braver, better, stronger…someone not me. When, in that blessed moment, I momentarily threw out the thoughts reminding me I wasn't good enough and gave myself over to the roar filling my ears, my body responded viscerally to the ocean's vast and powerful movement, knowing deeply I was meant to be there. The water washed over my toes, the sun flickered off the ocean in the distance, and I stepped into my sister's arms, letting my body take over where my mind could not; I had finally, ironically, gotten out of my own way so healing could begin.

If you've ever had a vibe or a "feeling," you've been on the cusp of whole-spectrum communication. As children, we tend to be most open to this kind of information and more fully aware of our intuition. Slowly, as we learn cultural codes ("smile and be polite, always") and digest unspoken social rules ("wear this not that, don't act weird, be cool") delivered by a frenzy of media, we close off our psychic and intuitive abilities. By the time we reach adulthood many of us have completely pinched off any sort of interior communication, instead opting to believe that intuition has no place in the "real" world. The next time you get a sensory feeling about something, take a moment, let the feeling wash over you, put your mind aside just for a few breaths, and see what knowledge emerges.

Consider that stepping into fear consciously and purposefully—listening to its message as we let go—allows us to care for ourselves on an essential level because when we stop running, choosing instead to look frankly at what we believe is so powerful, at what think we're so damned scared of, we begin to develop into the very courage we wish to embrace.

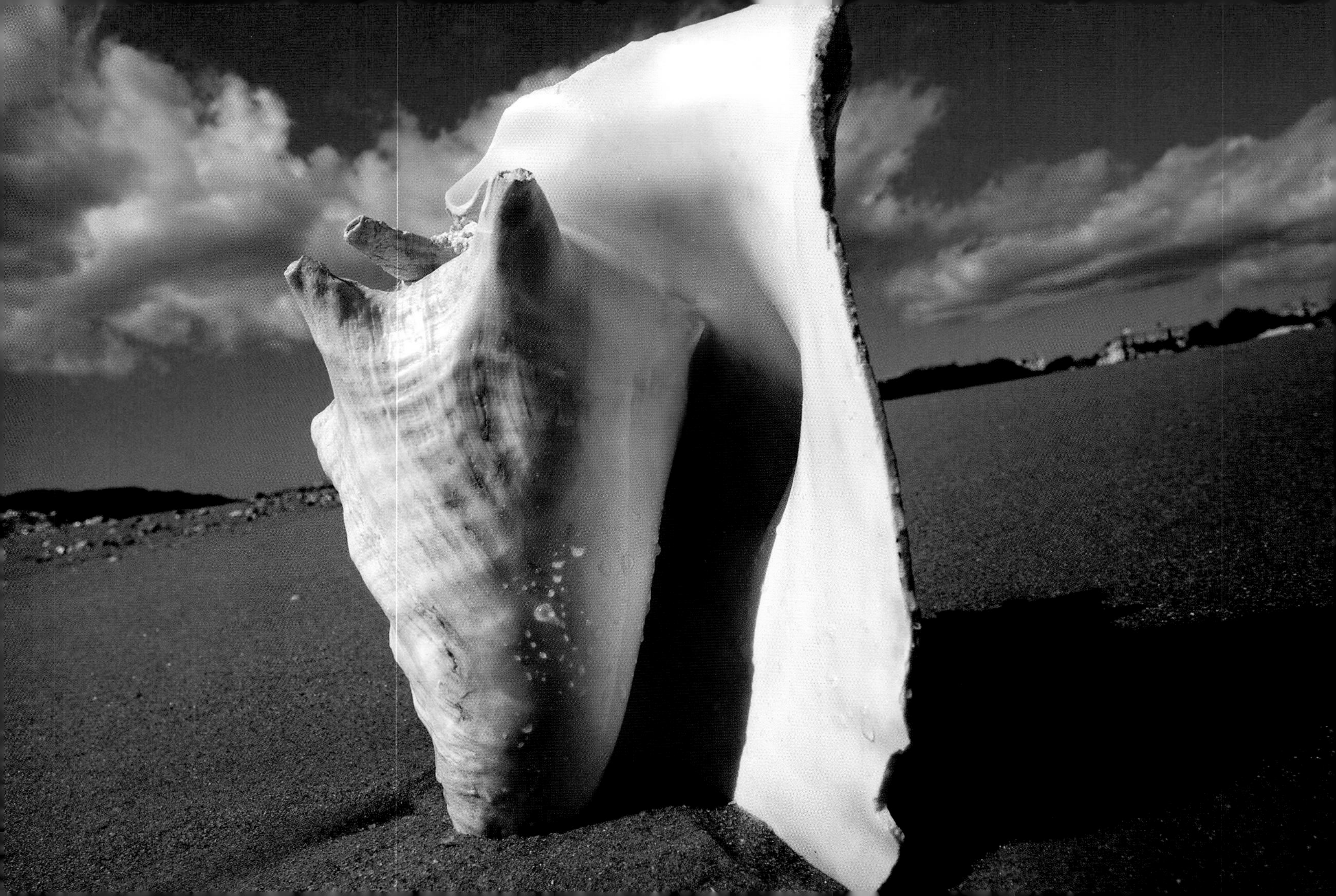

The Conch Meditation

You will know when the time has come for you to swap tired, suffocating fear for a new perspective. The opportunity presents itself to you as a brighter, clearer path. Feel the potential for amazing vibrancy, harmony, and success; indeed, these are already yours. Look at the fear honestly, and let it go.

Set Your Intention

Take a deep breath. Think for a moment about what thing in your life — what person, situation, emotion, or behavior — desperately needs deep exploration. The why isn't as important right now as the what. What do you avoid most? What might you gain when and if you choose to see and listen? Set your intention. An intention can be any statement, and should be stated in the positive:

I'm successfully…

I choose to let go of my pain.

I see my situation more clearly.

Whatever your intention, know that the gift of knowledge can be yours.

Breathe the Reiki Energy

Close your eyes and bring your attention to the area around your pubic bone, far below your belly button. Your first chakra, one of many energy centers, sits here, keeping you grounded and protected. Breathe deeply, in through your nose and out through your mouth, seeing your lower body fill with a beautiful red mist as your breathe. This grounding point keeps you in touch with the Earth while your mind and soul can take flight. Do this for a few moments. How does this feel? Are you scared? Nervous? Relaxed? Does the red mist have anything attached to it, like a sound or feeling? Without judging yourself, simply make note of whatever you notice, and then let it go.

Place your hands in front of you, on your abdomen. Breathe in, feeling the breath rise from your belly and chest into your shoulders, and exhale down into your arms, letting the breath move from your arms into your hands, and back into your body where your hands meet your lower belly. Feel each breath. Notice how the temperature of the breath changes during inhalation and exhalation. Your feet are growing roots deeply into the ground like a wise oak, connecting you to the earth. You may sway and totter, but you will not fall; you are one with earth, grounded and complete. Know that the earth holds you and connects you solidly and fearlessly to this life.

Move both hands from your abdomen to your heart, breathing slowly and deeply. Repeat your intentions to yourself with belief that they hold truth, and say the following with me:

All the power of the universe is here with me now.

Your message seeks you.

Visualize yourself comfortable and protected as you walk through a chilly breeze and overcast sky across a dark beach. The sand, damp and firmly packed, muffles your footfalls. The sea rumbles onto the jetty, sea-slick and darkened by pummeling waves, that sits directly in front of you. The huge, solid stones nestle together, making a grand throne for anyone willing to defy their edges. You peer into the crevices, feeling no fear. Wedged between two of the largest boulders, inside a space worn with time and coated with foam, you spot a beautiful conch shell, waiting. Brown and dull in shadow, the conch reveals an intricate swirling pattern and layers of color as you hold it up to the overcast sky.

You look deeply at the conch—white runs to gray, tan to black. One color fades as another begins in the circular pattern that spirals onto itself with no beginning or end. Waves batter the jetty, splashing you with spray; although you feel the torrential force of the sea only a few feet from you, know you are safe. Follow the conch's swirls with your finger, tracing the infinite pattern until you reach the conch's tip, its apex. You hold the sea's messenger in your hand, ready to receive its knowledge. Like an innocent and carefree child who has never known fear or reprise, judgment or pain, you hold the conch to your ear and listen. This message is yours.

What do you hear? Is the message pleasant or unwelcome? Inspiring or fearful? Be willing to listen truly and see deeply…

When you have heard all the conch has to say, place it back into its rock nest gently, where the sea will keep it safe. Thank the conch for its gift, and as a light rain begins to fall, dampening the already-wet sand and rocks, lift your face to the mist and smile at the gift you have just accepted.

Come back to the present and sit quietly for a moment. Bow your head for a moment of thanks, and feel peace and surrender.

What message did the conch have for you? Was it easy to hear? Hard to digest? Without judgment or fear, take a moment to write it down in a safe and private place.

Now write down three affirmations of your own creation, concentrating on addressing fears you have in the past avoided, but will now look at fully and clearly. These are fears you will overcome. Leave behind all the ugly judgment that says you can't write or it won't be good enough. These affirmations are for your eyes only, and come from the deepest part of yourself. Take a breath, give yourself a moment, and they will come. What do you want most? What scares you? What do you really need? Write it down in the form of an affirmation. They may be as long or short, as dramatic or plain as you like. State them in the positive, for example "I am feeling braver each day about my swimming lessons," versus "I'm not scared of swimming anymore."

Each morning before you pop in contacts, gulp down coffee, or shake open the newspaper, say one of these three affirmations to yourself. The choice is yours. Repeat your favorite affirmation to yourself each day and, if you can, throughout the day. Affirmations actually help to reprogram our thought patterns, so treat them as a healthy snack, something that's yours alone, to be enjoyed with no guilt.

After thirty days, revisit these affirmations honestly. Has anything changed? You've created a fissure in your fear—what do you see in that crack you've made? What do you believe would happen were you to blow it wide open? Even if behaviors haven't changed yet, your thought patterns have, and you now know the actions you need to take. Knowledge is powerful, and action follows thought. Your actions, big or small, directly impact and create the result that is your life. Whether you've wet your toes at the ocean's gentle edge or jumped right into the roaring abyss of a wave, your actions create ripples. What you have affirmed is right now, in this moment, determining your actions and creating magnificent personal power![6]

Shells & Bells

The innermost whirl of a conch—its "columnella"[7] or heart—has a power all its own and, in rougher tidal areas, can often be the only piece of conch left when it reaches shore. Of all the shells and quartz I have collected over three decades of scanning jetties and tidal basins, my favorites stand out: two bumped and bruised columnellas that washed up to me as I stood at the ocean's edge. Columnellas reflect back to us the highest qualities of our heart chakra, the center from which the essence of our passion, wholeness, tolerance, and acceptance of life pours. A form of absolute power and strength, tossed and beaten by the sea, the columnella withstands amazing rigors to make its way to the shoreline. Busted but beautiful, columnellas are no less than living analogies of our souls.

25

Conch Affirmation

I whole-body hear the Conch's communication.

This knowledge protects and blesses me.

Scared but able, I see the Truth of myself.

I face fear: scarred, clear, and True.

Embracing
Forgiveness

By the time Mermaid's Purses wash up with the tide, their occupants
have gestated and left for the sea, leaving behind unique casements.
These spaces, like our bruised and unforgiving hearts, once held life.
What does it require to reclaim those empty places in our hearts, making
them again the source of light and love? Some traditions claim that
forgiveness is the only path that allows us to live with inner peace. What
choices must one make in order to live wholly within the possibilities
and limits of forgiveness? Making the choice to forgive—especially
ourselves—means creating a place where compassion and freedom
meet, where the human condition lives healthy and whole.

Fear and shame burn in my throat. I look on silently as my dad lies halfway between the kitchen and dining room, face-down on the carpet where he has passed out. I see the quick shudder pass through him from where I sit at the kitchen table, notice the funny, glazed stare, and then watch him fall.

My eight-year-old mind spins with terror, followed by immense relief when I realize he can't scream at us if his mouth is buried in carpet. I look at my mom, expecting her to turn at the sound, to notice, to do something. She hasn't heard. Quietly, I pick up my math books and head upstairs to my room, my stomach twirling and spinning. I stand just inside my door, knuckles pressed white against my teeth. Is he dying? Already dead? The fleeting relief feels sick against my raw fear. No sound comes from the kitchen. Hasn't my mother seen him yet? Maybe he got up and walked away...just got up and, embarrassed, walked right back into the den, the only room in the house with air conditioning, the room where we aren't allowed.

I creep down the stairs, the too-quiet making me dizzy. In the kitchen my mother stands at the sink, stuffing a chicken, unaware of him lying a few steps from her. Even at that age I recognize the bizarre disbelief of the situation. Carefully, I move to the table.

"Mom, Dad seems sick."

"Hmm?"

I point a shaky finger. "He's passed out or something." Or something. Maybe he's dead. It's my fault for not telling sooner. How long had it been? Following my pointed finger, my mother cries out and springs towards my father, cradling his head and whispering in his ear. I stand by, helpless, guilty, scared he has died, wanting him dead. Then I hear her say it to his unconscious face.

"I'll leave! Don't do this! This just isn't worth it! I'll go! It's all my fault!" Her fault? I stand with my mouth hanging open as my mother screams for the phone. As he slowly wakes in her arms. As she tells my father—the abuser, the cheat, the gambler who will eventually boot us from our home—that his stress is her fault. I can hardly walk as I grab the phone from the hook and hand it to her.

He comes home from the hospital that evening. The diagnosis had been innocuous—a faint caused from the heat. I watch him stride back into the air-conditioned den, note his watery eyes and yellow pallor, hear him bark for iced tea. Eyes down, I deliver the tea and escape quickly. I flee upstairs and crawl into bed, hugging my stomach now shooting with pain. My mother's words have left me clueless and unforgiven, guilty of some transgression I can't even name. Exactly how have we created this? I cannot fathom how my mother, and by extension, I, have made my father sick. I sit and swallow my shame and hate, wondering how to negotiate this tsunami, unable to see what I have done to create such confusion and loathing.

I recall this story with both shame and horror as, at my counselor's prompting, I scribble illegibly down the length of a legal pad all the reasons I cannot possibly write a book chapter on the importance of forgiveness. Even more absurdly, this chapter will help others achieve peace surrounding old hurts. How can I, grossly flawed as I am in this area, even consider helping someone else lift the burden of unforgiven wounds? Retreating into self-righteousness or, even worse, apathy, I've more than once failed to negotiate forgiveness. I'm easy to anger, tend to hold grudges, and forgive slower than honey dripping from a spoon.

Reiki Master or not, I suck at this.

The shame of being unable to discuss forgiveness, of failing to prescribe a way of achieving this elusive peace, feels rooted in my own fear. Do I need to be religious, someone like the Dalai Lama, to talk about forgiving? Worse, do I look like a hypocrite when discussing forgiveness, the predictable friend who brims with good advice but never takes her own?

Some find it easy to move into forgiveness while others struggle terrifically with the concept, as well as the actual act. But many of these acts of forgiveness take place externally — gifts we bestow (or not) upon those who have wounded or slighted us. Before we can take this step towards compassionate humanity, however, we must first bandage our own hearts.

Unsure of my path, leaning over my legal pad in shame, not knowing what I can possibly offer my readers in this chapter, I remember with piercing clarity my mother kneeling by my father that bizarre Sunday afternoon, claiming our volatile, abusive lives were her fault and, by association, mine. While I had always suspected I had a role (hazy and uncertain it may have been) in creating our scary, hellish home — presumably such a place could only exist because I was broken and disgusting myself — I had never heard it spoken so plainly and openly. Her claim marked me deeply that day and not until I began scribbling on my legal pad did I realize that before I could even begin considering forgiveness for my mother or father, I needed to forgive myself.

Self-forgiveness has always come slowly for me, like trying to thaw ice cubes in the freezer — a painfully frustrating enterprise. In my Catholic school growing up we were taught to love thy neighbor as thyself. For those beaten down by trauma, "loving thy neighbor," while sometimes stickier than we would prefer, still felt easier than taking a look within and staying for the show. Why would we put ourselves through the hassle of reliving the worst parts of ourselves just to forgive flaws and faults we spent decades tucking away out of the light? The answer lies in freedom. With self-forgiveness freedom comes to us in the most unique and valuable ways — freedom to live, breathe, move, and forgive others as well.

Martha Beck puts it beautifully in her autobiography of discovery in which she returns home to Mormon country only to unearth dirty family secrets of forgotten childhood abuse. Her ability to move past the pain comes in the utter freedom of knowing and forgiving herself, even at the expense of losing her entire family: "Whether or not my father had the freedom to choose his thoughts and actions, I do. I am free, and always have been; free to accept my own reality, free to trust my perceptions, free to believe what makes me feel sane even if others call me crazy, free to disagree even if it means great loss, free to seek the way home until I find it."[1]

While it may be hard to know if we are forgiving others properly and truly, forgiving ourselves first will allow us to

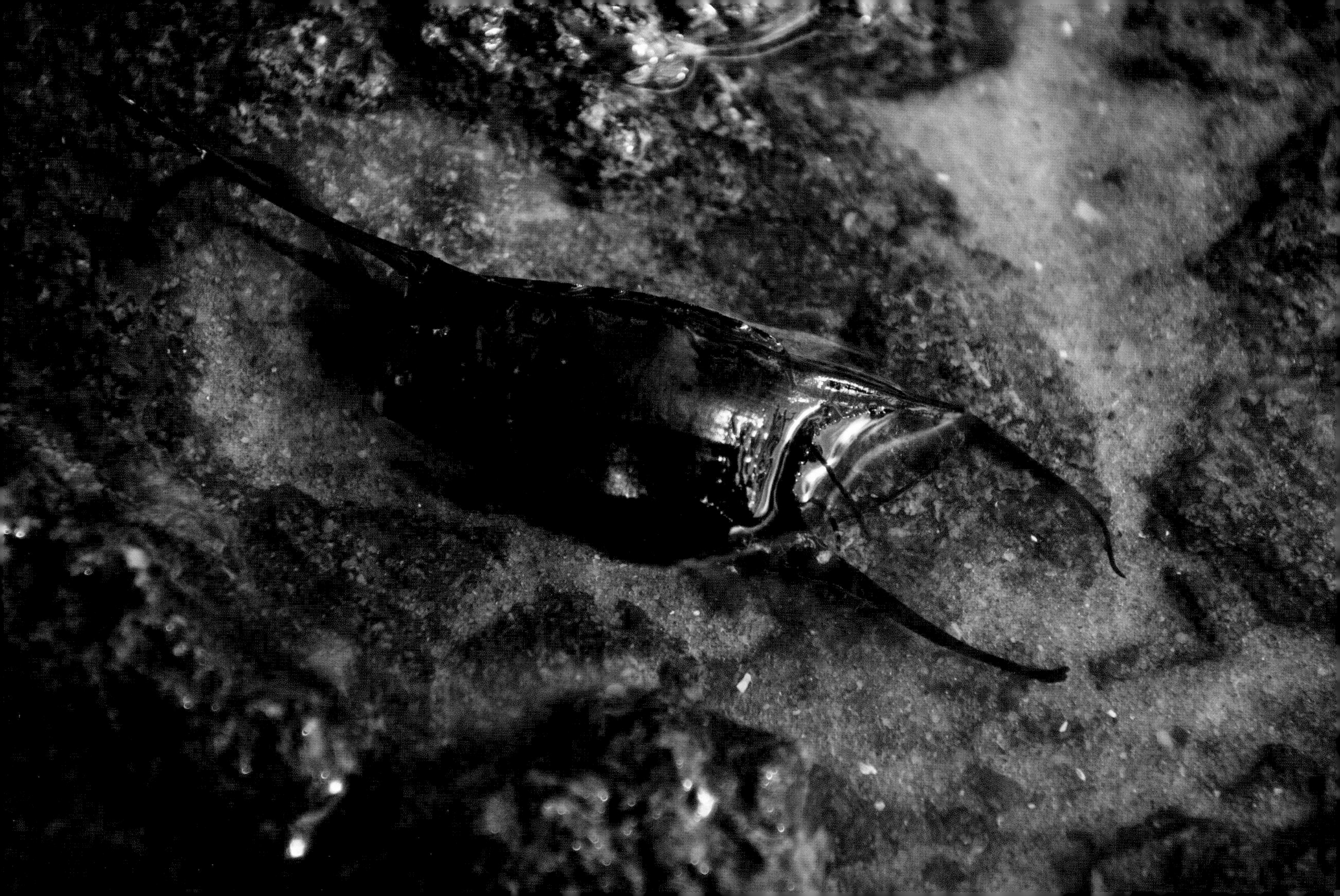

perform these other acts of forgiveness with a clarity we have not previously known. And how do we step into our own hearts and throw open Pandora's Box? Many of us, even those determined to enjoy healthy self-esteem and open, prosperous lives, usually don't seek out the gifts hidden in our own dirty laundry. Facing shame and guilt—the first, difficult steps to self forgiveness—loom huge and terrifying to the human condition; consequently, life (a generous benefactor of lessons) inevitably helps along this path by directing us into situations that demand attention, action, and of course, forgiveness.

I recently received an email from a colleague, a contributor to a controversial anthology of essays I am editing. This person, until then silent and presumably content, tersely stated that he found certain things about the anthology highly offensive. I felt surprised and hurt he would speak so glibly to me, his advocate, his *editor*, with such rudeness. After five years of working to unmask nasty policies endemic to higher educational, I had finally secured a publisher for these marginalized voices, enlisting a well known academic to write the Foreword. I had worked hard and consistently, by myself, to bring this project to fruition, and someone I barely knew felt free to call my choices—to call me—insensitive and offensive.

Wanting to be the bigger person, refusing to be rude in turn, I responded with understanding and respect. Since the anthology doesn't pay contributors beyond having their name in print, I gently invited him to withdraw his essay without penalty or hard feelings, reinforcing that I would understand. Hitting "Send" left me feeling proud I had been able to respond with gentle kindness and professionalism to someone who had treated me like a bad dog.

Based on the first email's bluster, I expected to receive a note confirming his withdrawal of the essay, and I felt fine about it....until he responded. Couched within a brief, stinging email, he again blatantly insulted me and *returned his publishing agreement*. He had not withdrawn his essay. Instead of standing behind his principles, withdrawing his essay, and shopping it elsewhere, he insulted me (again) *and* returned his contract, thus letting me know that while he still found my editorial choices offensive, he was willing to overlook them—and by extension, me—to get his essay published.

Was he kidding? I'm good enough to use to get published but not good enough to respect? Would he treat a *male* colleague this way? I doubted it. I ranted. I fumed. I wrote some of the nastiest emails I've ever constructed. After seeking the advice of a trusted friend ("Let it go. Leave his essay in and ignore him.") as well as a mentor ("You shouldn't cut him on the basis of his essay because it's not bad, but you *can* cut him for being a jerk."), and finding no peace of mind, I deleted the horrible emails I had not yet sent, stopped my fuming, and decided to give the situation careful thought outside of the hurt I had been feeling and the drama I had been feeding.

This man's behavior struck me as especially ironic in light of the anthology's topic: abuse, rankism, and higher education's easy exploitation of a gross and unequal distribution of power. I could cut him loose—my absolute and complete right as editor—but that seemed too pat, too superficial. I began to realize, slowly and with some unpleasantness, that had I not been so keyed into my *own* insecurity at being a first-time, female editor still smarting from her own brutal treatment by those in higher education, I would not have responded so viscerally to his complaints. I further realized I had let this contributor topple my confidence because his nagging, rude complaints startled me into facing my own fears of inadequacy and inability: What if there really were problems with this body of work? I had never before edited an entire anthology, worked with an overseas publisher, or been in charge of the international publication of highly controversial essays. What if the publisher recognized me as an imposter and withdrew its offer?

Despite a very real and palpable confidence built from many years of negotiating both publication success and rejection, there still existed the secret, niggling, leftover childhood suspicion that I was making a mess. And it bubbled to the surface with hardly any effort. No longer eight-years-old, holding my

stomach, feeling the storm of guilt and confusion swirl around me as I watched my father fall down and maybe die, I had a decision to make.

I reframed the situation. Realizing my own fear had driven my anger, that I had been working from a "child-centered woundedness"[2], I finally understood how little effort I wanted to waste on an inconsolable, low vibration action like fuming. Owning my own insecurity and feelings of victimhood put this contributor's—and my father's—behavior into a stunning new perspective for me. And with an expansion of my own heart by realizing how upset I still feel at having been used and abused by higher

Realizing MY OWN *fear* had *my* driven ANGER

education, I understood that I did not need to belabor one rude email.

I revisited more of my own painful memories, standing far enough away to give them some objectivity, and felt relieved at the discoveries I could make as an adult all these years later. I consciously forgave myself for the "stupidity" of being taken advantage of as a young instructor hungry for work. Instead, I renamed my untiring desire "dedication" and felt proud of my determination not to quit. I let go of the hurt at being "an idiot" to trust colleagues, and instead remembered myself as a girl with naïve hopefulness. And I tried to silence the nasty, judgmental voice that wondered how someone so educated, supposedly so bright, with so many jobs could still be so close to poverty on any given day.

I now better understand Martha Beck's experience, how we can give ourselves the truest gift of believing we are worthy—of being believed, respected, trusted, listened to, and loved. Of being able to forgive in our own way, own place, and own time. We can be free. And it begins in our own bruised but able hearts.

I still squirm when I think about my father lying on the floor, my thudding heart competing for attention with the cold metallic taste filling my mouth, and I hear my mother's claim…but I hear those words differently now. Thirty-odd years later, I can say with certainty I was the *least* broken of any person in that room, and my parents' marital problems were theirs, not mine, despite the way they had been continuously presented as something I should fix.

Now an old woman with advice on nearly every subject, my mother continues to support my father in odd, intimate ways that puzzle and confuse me. She still takes his calls, offers him coffee during his visits, and chats about long-ago friends. "Why do you do this?" I ask her. She shrugs and says what she's always said: "It's just the way I'm made."

Forgiveness, according to my mother, is nothing short of a necessity, something we must do for our own sanity so that we can "move on" though when I ask her what that means, she shrugs and confirms that amends must be made because, without the peace it brings, we "become sick or go insane with hate." Strong words from a woman who, in reality, has not really forgiven my father, but instead exhibits internal strength and compassion. Apparently, in doing so, she salves the wounds of she who needs it the most—herself—and for her, this is enough. My mother's perspective reminds me of poet Maya Angelou's view of forgiveness, how the act of forgiving oneself only makes us better and stronger such that much in the way "a diamond is the result of extreme pressure," the pressure of self-forgiveness "can make you something quite precious, quite wonderful, quite beautiful and extremely hard."[3]

Where does this all ultimately leave us when others hurt, abuse, insult, and damage us? Exactly where we started—understanding that the choice to forgive lies always, irrevocably, undeterringly with ourselves. Perhaps we forgive in a spiral, remembering, forgetting, undertaking to understand, eventually letting go. Or maybe we forgive in a straighter line, seeing the problem, releasing the anger, purging the issue and any hard feelings. And many of us don't forgive at all; we hold tightly, unable to let go of the pain, and refuse amends believing we are right and true to keep the grudge alive.

Regardless of where on the continuum of forgiveness we choose to place ourselves, our unwillingness to forgive others flourishes from the deep-seated choice not to forgive ourselves first. Imagine what it might feel like to experience that first blush of personal freedom, the relief that comes from making a choice that lets our own fear, hate, insecurity, and pain go. Maybe the Buddhists have it right; perhaps forgiveness is not necessarily absolution, but instead an opportunity to experience transformation.[4]

Embrace the potential of letting go of the pain and hurt, of forgiving those who have left you suffering, of releasing yourself. You are ready and able to forgive.

The Mermaid's Purse Meditation

You've felt the fear, born the hurt, and rallied against the pain—now it's time to let go, open your heart, and forgive. Before worrying about how well, how deeply, or how truly you can forgive others, make the choice to gift the person whose pain no one else can ease. Forgive yourself, and feel the world open itself to you.

Set Your Intention

Sit by yourself and close your eyes. As you breathe slowly, think about the people and experiences in your life who have left you angered, hurt, frustrated, or troubled. Has it been difficult to release this pain? If you find yourself holding a grudge, grasping at old hurts, refusing to let go of an incident or experience, where in your body has this emotional pain lodged itself? Breathe slowly into that place, and set your intention using positive language:

> I am strong because...
>
> I am whole because…
>
> I embrace forgiveness by….

If your intentions feel too big, too grand, too fake, then allow yourself smaller intentions that come closer to reality:

> I am stronger than yesterday.
>
> I feel more whole than I did five minutes ago.
>
> I am open to doing this meditation.

Just saying these intentions changes the vibration around you and begins to recreate your reality.

Breathe the Reiki Energy

Press your hands together as if in prayer and raise them into the heart area. Close your eyes and relax. Breathe deeply and slowly as you activate the heart chakra, the body's energy center that rules compassion and forgiveness. As you breath, see yourself clearly in your mind's eye as you look whole, loved, and uplifted. How would you feel without chains of self-judgment, with a lighter heart? Press each fingertip together once, slowly, breathing in and out with each press.

With each breath in, see a bright and vivid green energy flowing between your fingers, around your hands, and over your heart. With each exhale, cover yourself in a beautiful soft pink. Repeat your intentions and understand them to be irrefutable personal truth. Say the following with me:

> All the power of the universe is here with me now.

The sea awaits you.

Visualize yourself safe, happy, and at peace as you walk lightly upon a beach, the sand giving way gently under your feet with each step. The breeze feels warm and salty as it carries with it the last of the day's heat and sun. You come to the ocean's edge as dusk begins to fall and, with a light spirit, sink quietly into a still-warm hillock of sand a few feet from the pounding waves.

As your body begins to relax into the curve of warm sand, you notice that the tide is receding, moving farther away from you with every splash. Tiny sand crabs clamber over lost treasure that reveals itself to you, slowly and deliberately, one surge at a time. An expansiveness in your heart bubbles over at these gifts as bits of shell, seaweed, stones, tumbled quartz, wood, feathers, and damp sand offer themselves up to you. Tenacious Sandpipers begin running the waves, swooping in as a wave recedes to grab at insects in cracked sand crevices, scurrying back to land on tiny spindle legs as foam crashes and rolls towards shore.

By your feet, you notice a wet and bubbling chocolate-brown pouch with antennae-like edges along its four corners. You have found a mermaid's purse, and its inhabitants have already left to grow strong and agile in the sea. You pick up the purse, and get a sense of the life that has left this shell. You sit back in the sand, close your eyes, and hold the mermaid's purse delicately in your hands, feeling its smooth, wet texture under your fingers, smelling the clean salt air washing over you.

With your eyes closed and mind clear, recall a grudge you have held from a painful, unresolved disagreement. Breathing slowly, remember as many details of the incident as possible: What started the argument? Why did you feel angered? Did another person disrespect you? Ignore you? Hurt you in some way? Let the pain and anger gather and gain strength, filling your chest as you tense your muscles. When the memory has reached its limit, breath the anger and tension through your hands out into the mermaid's purse, filling it with your energy, knowing that it receives that which you no longer need.

As you exhale and let the tension flood from your body, your heart speaks to you with a clear and distinct message. You understand this message is yours.

Is the message made of words? Pictures? Colors? Does it hold advice or encouragement? Does the message carry a weight or energy? Accept your message without judgment.

When your heart has finished speaking to you, open your eyes and breathe deeply. Place the mermaid's purse at the tide line and watch as the next wave holds it gently — the way you now hold your own heart — and slowly carries it and your pain out to sea.

Stand slowly and bow deeply to the sea, thanking it for taking and transforming your pain. As you notice the dark blue bruise of dusk falling around you, know that the sea will always take away the flotsam and jetsam too heavy for our hearts to bear. Clasp your hands to your heart and bow to your higher self.

Mermaid's Purse Exercise

What message did your heart have waiting for you? Was the message pleasant? Difficult to hear? Inspirational? No matter what you heard, felt, or saw—images, sound, words, or something else entirely—write this message in a private place.

Over the next few weeks, pay attention to those moments when you feel frustrated, agitated, and angry, and how these feelings linger. When this happens, take a moment to write down what has caused this anger, whatever the source of agitation may be, without judging yourself.

After you have accumulated five incidents (this may take only hours for some people, weeks for others), look at your list closely while revisiting the message from your heart. What do the angry moments have in common? Does the source of your anger tend to be your own impatience or unwillingness? Who were you *really* angry with in the moment? Your heart has the answer.

Although we curse at bad drivers, hold a grudge when friends slight us, or even consider serious actions, like divorce, when a spouse hurts us, at the deepest and most profound level of our psyche, we tend to blame *ourselves*—for being too trusting, too kind, too open, too naïve, too stupid—and then we enter the world with closed hearts, impatience, anger, and frustration.

So while much of our anger and its accompanying behavior often stems from insecurity and self-loathing, we still always already inherently know what we need to live full, open, heart-filled lives. Even when rage fills us up, making forgiveness a lost and unlikely reality, our saving grace remains only a breath away…in our own hearts.

Mermaid's Purse Affirmation

I release anger, confusion, and doubt.

She holds my confusion, transforms my pain.

The ocean embraces what I no longer need.

I emerge forgiven, forgiving, whole.

Sharks & Skates

I step carefully over dried-out Mermaid's Purses as I walk the tide line, sometimes stopping to pick one up, their pointy tendrils and puffy casements no less fascinating for being long-empty of their living, fishy-filled insides. Sharks, skates, and rays—the more voracious and aggressive of the sea's ocean life—gestate like insect pupae inside these puffy, star-pointed casings. I feel nothing short of wonder the very first time I see one; Reiki, work deadlines, vacation—all forgotten in the midst of the ocean's bounty. My teen self in love with everything ocean-related comes barreling back to me and suddenly my adult world turns to grade-school science as I drop to the sand in fascination and begin studious examination right there in the shadow of the Cape May lighthouse. Only ever able to find dried-out husks, the likelihood of happening upon a moist purse, replete with innards and full of life, is slim. But if it ever does happen, I shall walk the living package out to sea, wishing and hoping that it reaches its potential, even if it did need a little help.

Dignifying
Grief

Though battered and beaten by the rigors of the sea, driftwood eventually comes ashore, beautifully weathered but whole. We too have the ability to step into our grief, eventually coming ashore weary but wise, bruised but intact. Grief, in all its pain and simplicity, often finds us when we are least prepared. But for a culture that shies away from discomfort of any kind, that spends millions on "quick fixes," are we ever really prepared? When we ask the universe for challenges and successes, sometimes we're answered in ways we could have hardly imagined, feeling like flotsam in a sea of pain and agony over our losses. Stepping forward to embrace our grief, though painful, helps us to be fuller, more complete individuals able to see the universe in broader strokes.

"I love your cut," I say to the woman in front of me as I stand in line at the craft store, gesturing at her hair. "You have really nice waves in the back." Her face lights up as she blushes a deep beet.

"Thanks. I just got it done." As we nod politely and approach our separate registers, I overhear her next words and at first think I am mistaken. But no, she has said what I thought.

"My son's grave, I'm decorating it…" she repeats to the woman behind the register. "He would have been five-years-old this week, so I do what I can, pick up odds and ends, things he would have enjoyed looking at." The clerk asks a question I can't catch, mumbles her sympathies, goes silent.

"We're told these things happen for a reason, but I don't know. I would have traded places, but it doesn't work that way."

Indeed, I think; it does not.

I peek over my shoulder at this woman, at her mixed bunch of silk flowers, some bright, some subdued, and feel a rush of deep affection for her, a stranger with whom I have spoken for no more than a few seconds. Deeply in pain, but moving forward through her grief, this woman is gracefully enduring a crushing blow, the kind we believe we could never face or even imagine for ourselves. And yet, when these tragedies strike us, we do endure them. We face these gaps in logic each day, moments when each and every detail of our lives disappears beneath a canopy of pain inflicted by some mind-blowing catastrophe. Many of us, like this woman, even manage it with grace.

Grief, an inevitability, will always appear in our lives despite all efforts to sidestep or ignore it, like the old casserole in the back of the fridge or dust bunnies under the bed. Many experience grief as a monster, a tidal force that beats us into submission while knocking us around the room. No wonder we often try to stifle the raw pain by burying it under a blanket of nonfeeling or wrapping ourselves in false security. While fake comforts like too much food, sex, and shopping—all addictions disguised as normalcy—superficially feel easy and look familiar, they actually bury and distort the most genuine and essential parts of ourselves a little more deeply.

Insulating ourselves in this way not only keeps the pain of grief from reaching us, but also makes it desperately hard to live genuinely from the heart. Without access to our own hearts, to the most fundamental places within ourselves, we live shallowly and vacantly, without deep connection to anyone, including ourselves. Too busy avoiding the pain, we strip ourselves of the invaluable opportunity to walk through the storm, bruised but whole, and recognize our innate power and resilience.

When we face horrific situations that make us curl into ourselves and require more than we feel able to supply to the world, then we have reached a time when we need to simply *be*. Let the body do its work…let the lungs breathe, the heart beat, the eyes blink. Sit with it. Be with the grief. While we might believe otherwise, grief cannot, will not, kill us. We can and, in many ways, already have lived through events we never thought we'd weather with sanity.

We tend to tell ourselves the very worst stories—those of lost hope and overwhelming despair, of inability and disgrace at weakness—when in actuality we often gain equilibrium much more quickly than we ever would have imagined. Grief seems to wield an ultimate power that strikes us down, but hope, buried deeply in our souls, fortifies and nudges us towards life when we feel there isn't anything left within. I won't claim that the wounds inflicted by our worst experiences will ever fully leave us, but releasing the pain into hope is a stunning next step. Simply, life goes on.

When I stitch all the jagged bits and pieces of memory together, I have a hazy recollection of standing in the middle of the room during the reception following my sister's burial. Denise had been a grown-up and married twenty-six to my fragile twelve. My second mother, my beach angel, my protector, now gone. I can barely wrap my mind around it. I am shattered glass; a strong look can flatten me. I beg my mother not to make me go to the funeral, not to have to bear any more of the staggering pain so publicly and openly, but I don't have the language to make my case. One look at my mother's face stops my words mid-sentence. I step into the solemn black limousine for the long, sickening ride.

The wake and funeral run together like a messy paint-by-numbers, but the reception stands out with clarity. I stand in the middle of the room numbly holding a plate of food and well up with disbelief, then quietly anxious rage, as some mourner I don't know smiles at a bit of conversation across the room. *Why the hell are you smiling? Don't you know my sister is dead?* Later that evening, the same feeling overwhelms me as I sit in front of a TV I don't watch, stunned that the studio audience can laugh. Don't they know what's happened today? I sit shocked and stunned that laughter still exists, that people on commercials still smile. I find it utterly inconceivable.

Many times during that sickening year—immediately after the funeral, during my parent's violent divorce a month later, after a traumatic car accident—I feel sure my heart will stop. The pain, unbearable and obscenely alive like something foreign using my mind as a host, overwhelms me. *No one can live through this*, I think. Who would want to? And yet, I do. I wake every morning, blessed with that blissful half-second before I remember why I haven't wanted to wake up at all. Somehow, even in all its glory, grief can't smother the tiny flame that lives deeply in my body, no matter how widely I prop open the door for hopelessness.

I feel this same soul-ripping loss twenty-five years later as I help to tear apart a thirteen year-long relationship with my partner. As the relationship shatters into the tiniest, sharpest fragments, I spend each day mourning that I haven't died in my sleep. I hold myself together, literally, with my arms wrapped around my knees, wondering at the monster I have become who, through sloppy mishandling of love, has created such a situation. Throughout the midst of this emotional agony, a perverse thought haunts me: Aren't I paid up against this? Haven't I already cleared this debt? I buried my sister all those years ago…and the Universe wants *more*?

"You're avoiding the pain," says one of my best friends. I puzzle over that. How am I avoiding pain when that's all I feel? I drown in it each day, my mind a twisted mess. The pain of knowing I helped along the destruction of this relationship courses through me, wrapping itself around me like a shawl.

As the demise of the relationship becomes clearer, my partner and I spend time at the ocean hoping to seal a huge fissure that has opened up to tear at us again. During this trip, I stumble out to my favorite jetty, bundled in a jacket and the wrong shoes, my partner a few paces behind me, and throw my helplessness wide. *Tell me what to do. Please tell me what to do.* I watch the waves roar and pound and seriously wonder if I'll ever feel sane again. Reiki seems so far from me that day, a healing power for someone else more pulled together and able to see clearly. As I close my eyes and wish I were dead, a rogue wave climbs the sand and soaks me to my thighs, splattering me back to reality even though moments ago the tide had been quietly rolling out. *Wake up!* the ocean screams at me. *Wake up and face this!* But I can't hear a word.

In the midst of my floundering, I confide in a knowledgeable and caring counselor who initiates me gently to the most startling information of all—that I have never sat silently with this pain, have never quieted my internal dialogue long enough to connect with any source of awareness[1]. My mental cacophony has held reality at bay all these months. In failing to accept and pay attention to the *actual grief of loss*, I focus instead on everything surrounding the relationship. I feel rudderless, stripped of all inner guidance.

I continue to court the pain daily, my inability to make a decision about my relationship with this man whom I love deeply but crookedly, creating more and greater levels of despair that become impossible to walk through clearly. Months later, tired of the interminable back and forth, my partner ends the relationship, leaving me with a deep sadness tempered by the oddest spark of relief. Finally, he has done what I could not.

Remarkably, the pain had never been the problem, but was instead a symptom of a much larger issue: fear. Fear of closure, of ending a period of my life, of saying goodbye, of re-evaluating my goals, and of recognizing that dreams we built together would not become reality because, as a couple, *we would not be*. Inundated with terror, I had failed to see pain as a signpost pointing me towards eventual sanity, if I could have just looked into its face. I needed to let go in order to move through it, to feel the pain that came with the deep knowledge that the relationship was over.

Yes, grief hurts. Tending our aching hearts gently is necessary; this ability and acceptance comes in time and with practice. One way to move through grief is to, well, *move*. The ocean presents the epitome of this, a roiling body in constant movement for centuries. She doesn't lodge in static complacency, but continually churns, grabs, and tumbles the flotsam and jetsam of our world. When we dignify grief with movement—even if our "movement" is to choose a deep stillness inside rather than scrabble after our loss—we create the space to heal. Human nature tells us to fear grief, to fear the drop into the very bottom of these feelings because we might drown in them and never rise again. Not so. "The way out is in"[2] because, without eventually touching the bottom of our intense feelings, our losses haunt us in odd bits and pieces forever.[3] When we pay attention to what is slipping from us or what we have lost, we surely go insane from the pain, but when we become still and face the grief, we can and do find presence, silence, and dignity.

Rather than getting caught up in trying to salve the pain, do the unexpected and *sit directly in the flow of what you are feeling*; embrace the loss in order to coexist with sadness rather then feel eaten alive by it. The moments during which we perform this embrace become apparent from the way they shine: During these times, we recall our child's favorite colors and decorate his grave with dignity, we step into the ocean and remember being held by someone whose love doesn't evaporate with their passing, we say goodbye to a lover and let go of brokenness with the hope of renewal. We grieve. But most importantly, we hope.

The Driftwood Meditation

Grieving doesn't wipe our slate clean, but instead helps us to move forward, elsewhere, in our pain. This meditative practice need not be precise nor perfect. Your simplest goal is *movement*, a nudge, a shift in what you feel at this very moment. Close your eyes and know this can be yours.

Set Your Intention

Close your eyes. Breathe deeply and evenly. Think for a moment about what deep-seated sadness keeps a hold on your heart. Have you lost someone or something close to you? Are you grieving the loss of life as it used to be, as it could be, as it may never be? Feel your lungs rise and fall, gently, evenly, slowly. Let your mind find quiet as the air moves into and out of your body. Set your intention using positive language:

I am whole and strong.

I will cry until I am cleansed,

and then I will stop.

I feel hope.

Perhaps your intention reveals a very simple need, like wanting to take one whole breath without hesitation or worry. Know that all intentions, large or small, become reality.

40

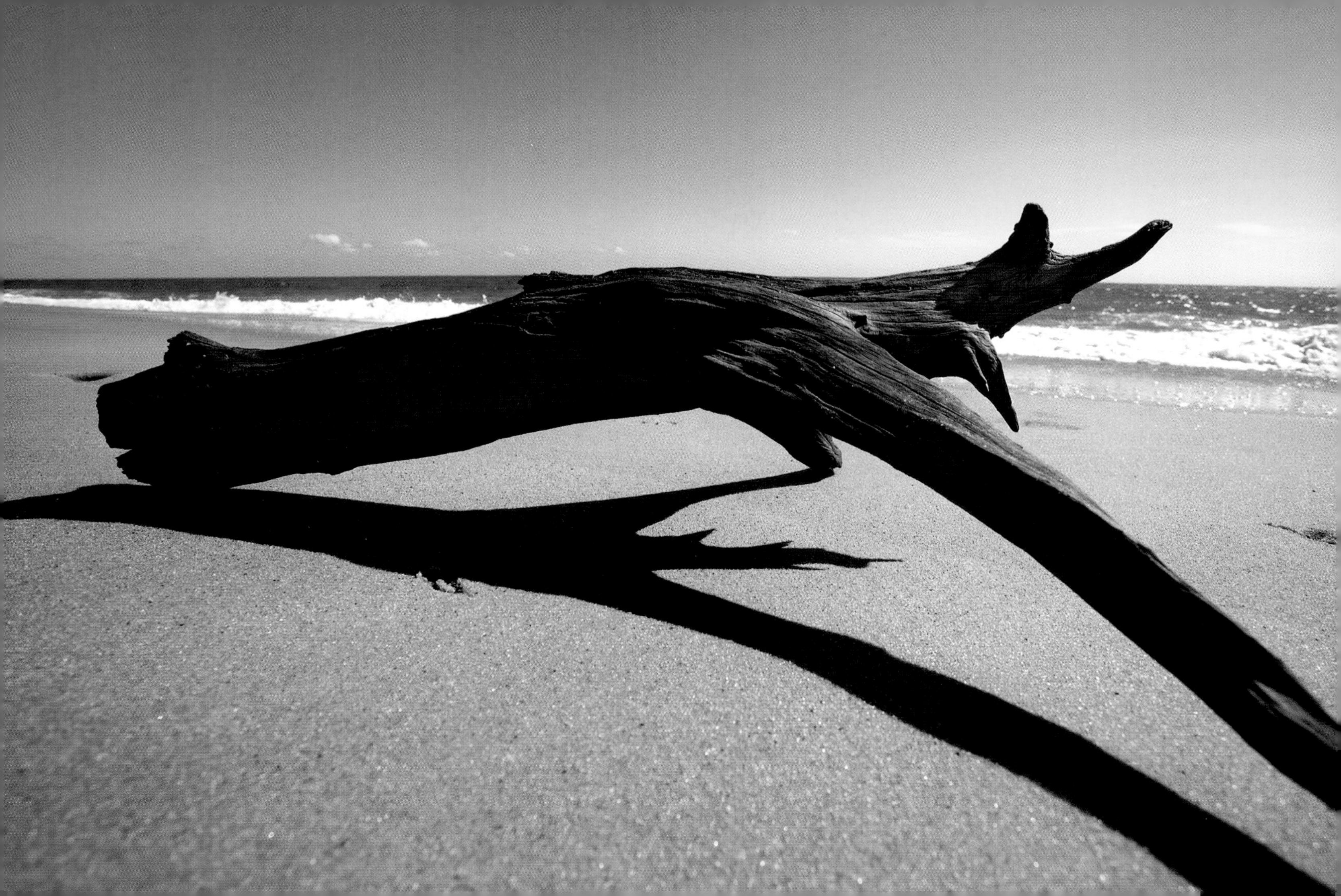

Breathe the Reiki Energy

Holding your hands together as though in prayer, rub them briskly. Feel the heat generated between them. Breathe deeply, pulling energy from your feet upwards through your spine as you inhale. Exhale the energy-filled breath audibly into your palms with a *whoosh*. This modified form of yogic breathing wakes the entire body. Repeat this, keeping your breathing deep and even. You are feeling God-energy, the Universal Life Force that infuses all of us coursing through your body right now. Visualize the breath and its energy trail radiating up your spine with each inhalation, then down your arms, and into your palms with each exhale.

Cross one hand over the other and place them both over your heart, radiating the energy right back into your body. Repeat your intention. Say the following with me:

All the power of the universe is here with me now.

The sea awaits you.

Acknowledge Your Message

Warm, protected, and whole, visualize yourself walking along the ocean's edge. The sun just begins to rise, throwing bright orange tendrils over the rim of the horizon. Foam bubbles by your feet as you step surely and firmly on the damp sand. There, ahead, among broken shells and a tangle of seaweed lies a small plank of brown, battered wood—driftwood thrust from the sea in a fit of tide. Blanched and slightly ragged, the wood invites you to pick it up and hold it for closer inspection.

Worn smooth and soft in places, shallow ruts and grooves pock its knotty face, giving it the appearance of an old and aged friend. The rising sun gives depth to its many indentations as it turns from caramel to tan, chestnut to oak in the shifting light. Notice its many dimensions—softness, hardness, worn spots, smooth planes, salty pockets. Though it looks battered and bruised, it fits the contours of your hands perfectly, feels whole. Bring the wood up to your heart as you stand on the ocean's edge. Feel its solid assuredness. Once part of something larger and stronger, something true and alive, this wood has now come to you with a message.

Listen to waves beating a rhythmic wash. Breath the salty air. Know you are safe and loved. Relax your heart into the wood. Turn the driftwood over in your hands, and read the message etched on its battered surface. This message exists for you alone.

What does it say?

Do you accept this message?

When you have digested your message, acknowledge the thrumming sea, the beach as it stretches before you, the sand that shifts under your feet. Thank the driftwood for its message and assistance. Place it back onto the sand, knowing you may come to this safe space at any time to receive a message from the Universe. Reach down and, as you brush your fingers in the cold sea, take a deep breath and open your eyes.

Come back to the present and sit quietly for a moment. Breath once more, sending love into your fragile heart.

Driftwood Exercise

Was the driftwood's message a statement? A question? Just one word? Maybe you were asked to do or feel something that seems impossible or difficult, or perhaps the message was pleasant and encouraging. No matter, take a moment to write it down in a safe and private place.

Over the next ten days, take just a minute each day to write down **one positive thing** you experience during that day. Maybe one day you did all the dishes, ate something healthy, or meditated for five minutes. Big or little, document these moments each day regardless if you think anyone else would consider them noteworthy. After ten days, look back over your list and see what you have added to your world, even if just to your little corner of it. **Ten days ago you hadn't done any of these things.** Repeat this exercise for another ten days, even if you don't feel like it. Take time to review the list and give yourself credit, even if you're feeling stingy or unkind towards yourself. Treat yourself gently. Take credit where it's due, even for the smallest of accomplishments.

By nudging your thoughts, slowly and surely, towards the recognition that you are actively adding to your world (rather than just taking up space in it feeling sad), your mind will eventually do this unconsciously. Grief, though it may sit like a little stone in our hearts for a while, need not be our defining factor. It can just *be* as we continue to move through our days, closer to hope and farther from despair with each step, each tiny action or accomplishment, each thought that says, "I am still here. And I am okay."

Remember, even the smallest steps nudge us forward and keep us moving and flowing with the shift of the tide, *even when it looks like we're not moving at all.*

Driftwood Affirmation

I trace the Driftwood path.   Water and sun leave me bruised but whole, weary but wise.

The Universe understands my fear and sadness.   I am awake and dignify my grief.

Sticks & Stones

Craggy and uneven, ugly and beautiful all at once, driftwood comes from all manner of places. Sitting in the sea for ages, once it hits the shore it might appear smooth, worn, lovely, or ragged. Driftwood holds a special, pure quality for me, and I know immediately if I should take it home when I've stumbled upon it. You too will know if a beach item would like to come home with you. If you are unsure, ask, and then follow the next feeling you get. Use driftwood the same way you would a crystal, placing it where it brings you peace or where it seems to want to go. If you don't have the luxury of being near a beach that regularly gifts its shores with driftwood, you might also enjoy working with crystals that heal the heart and root chakras. You might try rose quartz, aventurine, malachite, and rhodochrosite for your heart, and garnet, hematite, apache tear, bloodstone, and ruby for the root, as well as any others to which you are drawn. The possibility for healing using nature's gifts is endless.

43

Touching
Faith

"Cape May Diamonds"—clear quartz deposits that begin their 200-mile journey on the upper Delaware River—can spend thousands of years spinning and tossing in the surf before being nudged ashore at Sunset Beach in Cape May, New Jersey. The Kechemeche Indians, uninterested in selling the quartz to unsuspecting pawn brokers, instead took faith in the crystals' journey and beauty. When we become overwhelmed, understanding that no guarantee exists for our own safe landing ashore, we struggle with self-trust. Even when we're committed to our journey, we resist faith in ourselves, in knowing that we have the power to create change. Moving through these challenges depends upon embracing the power that comes from unconditional faith. We can heal ourselves if only we have the faith to surrender to the higher forces of good within.

"I make a slow turn around the back of the ring, seat high, heels down, toes in. Just as I reach the crest of the turn, I pull on the rein a shade too hard, pivoting my mount towards the jump. Mistaking my accidental shift for a command, the horse begins a butter-smooth canter towards the log jump, an intimidating three feet high. I feel her gather herself beneath me and spring forward to sail through the air.

My mind spins like a kite caught in a storm as, just before landing, I push away on my stirrups, lose my balance, and fly from her back, sending my hat sailing and snarling my foot in a stirrup. I am dragged ten feet before my confused mount stops. Bruised and terrified, I lay still and cry. I cram what I think I have just done far back into my mind and sift through my thoughts, landing on the easiest — the intense pain in my lower back.

Another rider rushes into the ring. "It's okay," I hear her whisper to the horse, "not your fault, baby." Of course not, I think. I take the burden. The mistake is mine: the shy, nervous girl who mucks stalls to pay for her riding lessons.

I still burn with shame when I revisit this adolescent memory, even now thirty years later. Everyone watching thought the horse would take the jump smoothly and I, a fair rider, would simply hang on. But I didn't, and the shame of it refuses to stay hidden any longer. I made this discovery a few years ago when some grand combination of being trapped inside an emotional maelstrom coupled with focused Reiki meditations unlocked the knowledge I had been sheltering. Finally able to voice my pain, I realize how that day's mistake had become an embarrassing metaphor for the way I approach life. The truth is unnerving and ugly: I pushed myself out of the stirrups. I actually threw myself from the horse as she took the jump *because I was afraid to go over.*

People guffaw when we talk of being fearful of success. *Who doesn't want to be successful?* In fact, many don't. Unable and unwilling to embrace the self-love and acceptance that comes with doing well and finding genuine happiness and satisfaction, some of us choose life situations that ensure safety, security, and just enough comfort so that we don't

reach past our false boundaries, even when we sit with nothing but sadness and unfulfillment. Many of us actively sabotage our lives, making choices and creating life paths that require months, years, and lifetimes of restitution. We lose all faith in ourselves and our abilities.

Much in the way we all cultivate different dreams, we also enter our life transitions with varying forms of acceptance. Some of us, delighted with the world's tricks, open ourselves to each new opportunity, welcome change, and embrace potential, facing each new challenge with a bright heart and calm spirit. Others of us, marred by unsafe childhoods, dig in firmly while regretting our inability to move forward. Sometimes, unfortunately, our only movement comes out of desperation, by force, or from a kick in the pants.

What I call "My Life, Part II" began in 2006 when my partner, of thirteen years, and I split. The break-up had a horrific cascading effect as, over the course of a few months, I moved three times, left secure full-time work, and discovered that I am not the woman I believed myself to be. I spent the entire year riding the wheel of destiny, discovering new life paths, new ways of surviving, and new life routines, all against my conscious will. Throughout it all, despite my Reiki training, I felt completely bereft of higher spiritual guidance. Like a tiny rowboat tossed into turbulent seas, I lived without faith or hope.

Finding faith, that sense of confidence and security that lets us know *everything will be fine*, seems easy enough at face value, and perhaps it is for those raised in functional homes, but I certainly never had any clue what it felt like. My beliefs have always run more along the lines of Murphy's Law—things will always go wrong because that's how life works; if things go right, well, that's almost worse because I'll be expected to pay up for that joy at a later time. Those who grow up with trauma, who experience a childhood rife with confused adults creating painful situations, learn quickly that lives without confidence or joy tend to equal safety. We choose failure—we throw ourselves from the horse at the peak of the jump—believing we deserve nothing, that success

and health and peace of mind will always elude us, that avoiding what we want is safest since anything we may achieve will inevitably be lost or taken. We become adept at turning faith aside and expecting nothing. Sadly, our lives evolve into a series of pessimistic clichés, and we don't even know it.

Living FROM A place *of* faith DEMANDS trust... *&* change.

Living from a place of faith demands trust…and change. An acquaintance of mine called them *endbeginnings*—powerful periods of time and space in which we are ushered, often against our will, into a deepening of our evolving selves. We've all been forced from our comfort zones by work, health, family strife, and life in general in ways that have left us dangling over emotional cliffs. But consider, beyond the screaming discomfort and the aggravated exhaustion, what that ultimate resolution felt like. Things changed and you survived. Happy or not, just believing that some outcome is waiting, and that it will be okay—that you *can* handle it—is faith.

Finding faith, in its many varied versions, involves unlocking a loving power much greater than ourselves. This same power guides the greater design and purpose of our lives and helps us negotiate the daily events flowing from dramatic changes and losses when our hearts hurt and we feel empty. I still crave many things…financial stability, a home of my own, forgiveness. While a wavering skepticism used to keep these desires at arm's reach, convincing me that nothing in my life would ever pull together into anything remotely close to success or achievement, I now understand firsthand how a gentler, kinder, and more faith-inspired mindset brings me closer to my dreams.

As I grew up and began to write my stories down, I saw how self-discovery, like the writing process, can't be forced or cajoled. Instead, faith in oneself comes from a space that humans, in our many confused moments, simply try to embrace. I couldn't demand it. Instead my writing helped me gain a different perspective, one I hadn't had while trying furiously to make sense of a crazy and unstable home.

Ironically, faith is often tested at those very times when its presence feels most crucial, like those days when depression or hopelessness haunt us. If we can figure out how to awaken our own faith within, we have the ability to recognize that our pain, discomfort, confusion, and despair **will** inevitably shift, that despite the daily missteps that snatch stability from us, the pain hooked into our hearts will eventually lose its grip. We only need to recognize faith's momentous capacity to experience it; it buoys us up, connects us to others, and helps us maintain sanity during those moments when we feel barely able to help ourselves.

I still remember that unsettling day… I shift in my chair and scrawl another STAY/GO list, three weeks into my first disastrous semester of graduate school. I look down: Six bullets under GO, two under STAY. Not good. Two lousy reasons to stay at graduate school, and six reasons to leave. According to my columns, I should start packing. But I don't want to go just yet. I decide a good place to begin reaffirming faith in myself is to stop making GO and STAY columns during 16th Century Literature, my most hated class.

Although I adore the idea, attending graduate school creates more problems than seem solvable at first. Like my mother. When I ask for help with financial aid forms, she suddenly can't remember how they work, telling me I'll have to get help from someone else. Rather than speaking openly and plainly, letting me know she's crushed at my choice to leave her for a school seven hours away, she just pretends I'm not going. Obviously in pain and unable to let go, my mom's stubbornness unlocks a determination in me I haven't felt in years.

After loading the U-haul and finally pulling away, I feel elated, but also something else, something familiar — *late*. I am late, out of sync, too old. I should have left home five years ago like my friends, when I was a Freshman. Instead, bowing to family expectation, I chose the same expensive private university my brother had attended and, barely scraping by on student loans and three part-time jobs, commuted for four miserable years, trying desperately to fit in. But as I try to begin a new life, a happier, better, different one from that I've left behind, unbelievably, all I want is my mom. This makes me feel remarkably stupid.

About a month into my hated class, I am scheduled to teach a class session as an assignment. I numb my nervousness with a shot of rum and a glass of wine around 9 AM. At 9:30, I strive for composure as I deliver my lecture. I've prepped for days and want the lecture to go perfectly and, to my surprise, it does. I stop by my professor's desk after class, glance down into his grade book, and notice he has given me a check-minus, the equivalent of an "F." He turns to me and follows my wide eyes down to the grade book, which he snaps shut.

"You lectured," he says matter of factly.

I stand, stunned, my mouth open, the rum finally kicking in. I did exactly what teachers have done throughout my whole school career: I lectured. Wasn't I *supposed* to lecture? Isn't that what teachers *do*?

Eventually, over the next ten years as I discover my passion for the classroom, I learn how to nudge class discussion, move it here and there, teaching as though I were throwing a piece of pottery, gently but firmly, never forcing, letting excess fall away, allowing what remains to take on the quality of something special. But at that moment—totally buzzed on rum and wine, clueless that someday I will love teaching—I am devastated. And I've failed the damn assignment.

Later in the week, I compose myself, seek him out, and ask about my poor grade. I am shocked to find he doesn't even know my name even though our class has fewer than ten students. But

then he really stuns me when he says I lacked innovation and threw away all opportunity to be "interesting." He shakes his head, sharing his disappointment at my lack of creativity as a teaching assistant…which I am not. I hurry to explain. I'm not a teaching graduate student, but rather a work study who does secretarial work across campus in exchange for financial aid. I have not taught before. Ever. So without knowing what else to do I had followed *his teaching style*, lecturing the same way he lectures at us every class period. He remains skeptical. "I expected something more original," he says, smirking.

I leave his office in tears, confused and devastated. As I walk home, I wonder at the ludicrous lies I must have told myself to believe I could do this. Why I ever assumed I could be successful in graduate school next to grown up students who actually teach other students and talk about literary theories I've never heard of. What about my miserable undergraduate years, so full of unhappiness and bullshit, had led me here expecting something better? What an idiot! I have no faith

in anything—in fairness, in what I'm studying, and especially in myself.

I am a complete and total loser.

Two weeks later, I stare at the huge and remarkable red "A" scrawled across the last page of the Stephen Crane paper I've written for American Lit, my very favorite class. I resist the urge to scream or run as something snaps into place. I don't know what I'm feeling. Relief? Hope? Happiness? I'm not sure, but something niggles at me.

I remember the feeling of pure wonder I experienced six weeks earlier walking in my very own apartment for the first time. I rewind to the letter announcing my acceptance into the program. I recall slinking into my mom's bedroom to tell her about graduate school, how my fingers traced the deep walnut scrolls on her dresser as I explained that I want something I've never considered for myself, an underachieving college student too afraid to ever really try.

Right there, in the middle of Williams Hall, gaping at my perfect red "A," I decide to stay in graduate school and face my fears. The paper is only one assignment, but it's representative, my shiny new metaphor, and I'm not going home. I am *exactly* where I am supposed to be. I hope fiercely that I don't fail horribly. I might even be okay. And I firmly push 16th Century Lit out of my thoughts. A few weeks later I stumble across the quote by Saul David Alinsky, and feel something twist inside:

> "When written in Chinese, the word 'crisis' is composed of two characters – one represents danger, and the other represents opportunity."[1]

I step outside my apartment with the Alinsky quote wrapped around my thoughts and gaze at the Blue Ridge mountains in the distance. The view soaks into me. I have chosen to be here for myself. This knowledge — this faith that has always been mine to own — will sustain me through exams, a frightful term paper, and my decision to end a loving but not-quite-right relationship.

I want to become someone I used to know, a girl with huge dreams she tucked away but never forgot. Those dreams used to ripple with an energy of their own before being suffocated under fear and doubt. I felt just about every emotion and encountered every possible situation that semester — panic attacks, adult chicken pox, a compulsively lying new best friend, assignments I didn't understand — and faced the fear by actually trying my best instead of expecting the worst. I chose to have faith in myself.

Faith asks us to move forward before we know where the journey will end. Depending on one's belief system, this may demand a trust in God, the Goddess, the Universe, humankind, fate, or any number of higher powers, but mostly and irrevocably, this demands a trust in *ourselves*. This trust, in turn, manifests itself in confidence, self-love, hope, and even productive fear. Investing in faith leads us to a place of authenticity, of trust deep within ourselves where we may pursue self-knowledge without manipulation, dishonesty, or apathy. Once we choose to have faith — essentially choosing to believe in ourselves — we dissolve the artificial boundaries between our material and spiritual selves.

How do we step over the lines we draw for ourselves, those arbitrary boundaries we use to determine comfort and success? How do we find the faith to keep moving forward? By living in the present. *My life right now is fish heads and coffee grinds,* I say to a friend, *I hope you'll bear with me as I find my way through to the other side.* As we reach forward past old hurts and pains, past the smelly fish heads and coffee grinds that make up our daily trash, we eventually find some clarity. Maybe not all at once, and maybe not perfectly at first, but we do. Shoving away the terror that strangles our potential, we may stumble and will very likely feel scared all over again. This is okay. We start to understand our own potential, that we *can* get that special job, find a loving partner, have the child we always wanted, succeed at that seemingly impossible task. We can. And we will!

Annie Lamott has said that we need to make messes to find out who we are and why we're here. So many years of faithlessness have finally given way to wanting something better and greater, and in order to do this, I have chosen

to trust myself. I do this by stepping, face forward, into the mess everyday. When we embrace this simple belief—*I am fine right at this moment. I have faith in myself*—we begin to treat ourselves with the same respect we usually reserve for others, a shock for those of us who often feel we're not good enough.

When the Kechemeche stepped across the rocky dunes of Sunset Beach in Cape May, lifting and sifting out glistening pieces of quartz from the gentle bay shore, they celebrated, believing they had uncovered totems of good luck and fortune. Once prospectors found the quartz, however, its value shifted dramatically. No longer just a good luck charm, the same quartz, with some polishing, took on new value as a "Cape May Diamond."

Like the quartz tumbling their way down the Delaware River, rolling in the surf for years, pushed by bigger and greater forces, we too fall into daily, involuntary patterns, forget where our values reside, and turn from our spiritual sides, from self-love. What would our lives look like if we lived from faith-based intuition? Built for the most part on pragmatism, fortitude, and hard work, our lives depend upon faith as one of its most basic foundations. We take steps demanded by faith every day when we leave our homes, drive a car, move forward through our day, and put our lives and futures in the hands of doctors, bosses, teachers, police officers, and myriad others upon whom we rely in many ways, small and large. Viewed through this lens, faith becomes less daunting and more accessible, something anyone can have.

Sometimes, we just have to look for it and allow ourselves to have it when we find it. Although some days I stumble clumsily, I still know I am exactly where I am supposed to be.

And so do you.

The Quartz Crystal Meditation

Finding and holding faith in our hearts allow us to take steps on our most necessary journeys despite pain, confusion, and impossibility that seem to trip us as we make our way. Quartz magnifies and expands intention and power; this meditative practice asks you to surrender, have faith, *believe*. Close your eyes and feel your full heart.

Set Your Intention

Sit quietly, breathing deeply and evenly. Where in your life do you lacking faith? Do you tell yourself stories around certain incidents or experiences that underscore a lack of trust in your world and the Universe? As breath moves into and out of your lungs, know that your faith in the world has never truly left you. You merely need to rediscover it, let light find it, give it air again. Set your intention using positive words and thoughts:

I know all will be as it should.

I give myself over to trust.

I know divine guidance watches over me.

The faith is already yours, waiting for you.

Breathe the Reiki Energy

Cross one hand over the other and place them both over your solar plexus area, the space below your ribs and above your navel. Breathe slowly, with eyes closed, feeling your stomach rise and fall with each breath. Do this for the length of five breaths, making each inhalation and exhalation just a tiny bit longer each time. Scan your body, noticing places that feel stiff, tight, or stuck. Breathe into these spaces, letting your breath lead you as you repeat your intention. Say the following with me:

All the power of the universe is here with me now.

The sea awaits you.

Acknowledge Your Message

You feel complete and utter peace as you visualize yourself walking slowly along the shoreline of a quiet bay. The scent of brine and salt reach your nose and bring with it a feeling of total calm. As you step into the late afternoon light, the sun casts a soft shadow onto the tiny tidal washes that gently touch the shore without the fury of ocean waves. You move into a gentle surf that covers your feet, noticing the way your toes sink and shift in the sand. Tiny grains of sand slowly give way to larger and bigger stones, tumbled round and smooth in the light surf, until you are walking on what seems to be a soft bed of river rock. Brown, grey, blue-tinged, white, cream, light green…each stone captures your attention with its loveliness.

Among the many varied stones that shift under your weight, you spot something special shining in the surf, like a lost pirate's treasure. The fist-sized quartz looks cold and solid, heavy and dense. You want to hold this stone, feel its power and weight, but it's just a little too far away in the water, a little too special for you. Round and tumbled, the mineral shines like a small mirror.

You step towards the quartz and feel the stones beneath your feet shift. You can see the stone before you, but still cannot see past the ocean foam, cannot tell how shallow or deep the bay may be. Safe, secure, and unconditionally loved in this moment, able to embrace the unknown, you step forward and pluck the quartz from the ocean tide with a feeling of power. You are free of fear and hesitation.

Hold up the quartz. In and amongst its fissures and inclusions, there is a shape. You now hold your own faith, once dulled by fear and hopelessness, in your hand. The quartz is your gift. The message is yours.

Your deepest faith lies within the stone. What do you see? What shape does your faith take?

Hold the quartz close to your heart before laying it down gently, close to the tidal pool's edge. As you watch, the bay waters gently retrieve it to continue its journey.

Come back to the present and sit quietly for a moment. Bow your head for a moment of thanks.

What did you see within the quartz's depths? Is internal resistance trying to push the message away? Perhaps your thinking mind tells you that the message couldn't be true, that your imagination has just made it up. Today, though, you will have faith in yourself and your ability by making note of your message, no matter the resistance. Take a moment to write it down in a safe and private place.

On a piece of blank paper, write down one life dream you would like to accomplish. Perhaps you want to lose weight, write a book, return to school, or find strength to change your life. No matter how outlandish or unreachable your dream may sound, write it down.

Each evening, take a quiet moment for yourself. Regardless of whether this lasts as long as it takes to soak in a luxurious bath or as short as the span of one focused breath, make the moment yours, completely and totally. Take out your paper and look at your dream. Write down one thing you can do to help your dream move into reality, and say to yourself, "This is possible." Your list may be populated with action items that seem hard, impossible, improbable, and maybe even ridiculous to your doubting mind in the moment, but continue to write them down, leaving judgment behind. *This is possible.*

After thirty days, look at your dream goal and the list of action items that will help to move this dream towards reality. What do these items have in common? Have you taken action on any of them? *Can you do one of these items today?*

Perhaps you've reached that goal of losing a few pounds or making peace with a family member. For most of us, though, achieving a dream will require time, patience, and faith. Look back at this list often, adding and subtracting items as needed. Thirty days ago you could barely acknowledge having a dream. Today, you possess the knowledge that you can move forward on your path of self-love and trust at any time! You have found faith in yourself. *This dream is possible.*

Crystals & Clarity

Considered the "plain Jane" of the mineral world, quartz quietly amplifies the effects of stones and intentions in subtle but powerful ways. Much different than the polished quartz found in gem shops, the beach quartz I collect along the back bays and ocean fronts of Cape May has been worn smooth by tidal current and comes from the ocean frosted, solid white, or dappled and clouded with minerals deposits. As children scour the beaches for that perfect shell, I hone in on the rocks, asking each piece if it would like to come with me before popping it into my pocket. These crystals sit on shelves, in my car, along my writing space and all over my home, insinuating themselves into my life as watchers and amplifiers. The next time you stand near water, whether it be an ocean, back bay, river, lake, creek, or even puddle, look for that rock that sings out to your heart. It waits for you.

Quartz Affirmation

The quartz mirrors my need.

I see and accept whole-self possibility.

The inclusions create my path.

Faith guides my Truth.

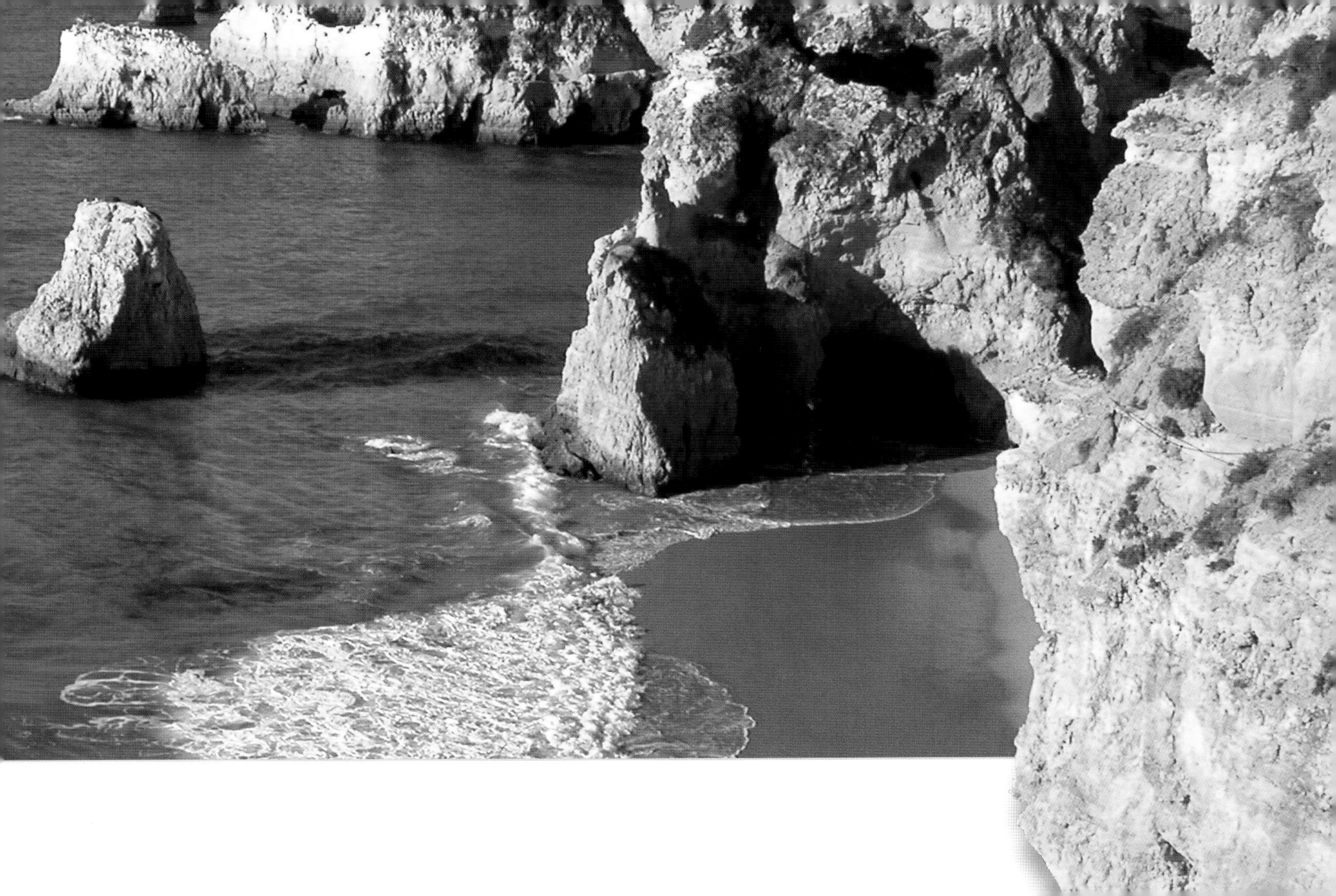

Alchemizing

Hope

Just as precious and rare sea glass begins its journey as refuse with an accidental destination, we too can transform, remember our worth, and rediscover the hope, beauty, and light that makes up our souls. Though we may not realize that thoughts, dropped into the world with casual indifference, have any effect on our lives, we do in fact create the world we see. Affirmation, intention, and determination affect our lives in powerful ways. The many wondrous, inherent powers we possess—intention to intuition, healing energy to prescience—are available to us but often remain untapped. Letting go of our learned need to rationalize each thought and rediscovering the imagination wrung from us as children brings us closer and deeper to our soul's purpose, to a future of hope.

I look around the dull cubicle and sigh. The softly padded cubicle walls, a bland brown-gray, separate me from an equally dreary aisle. Whispered bits of conversation float around the room, punctuated only by an occasional ringing phone. I sit under the pulsing fluorescent lights and resist a headache. I want to cry. The pleasant anticipation I usually feel in a new job are absent. Instead I am leaden and bone-tired, and it's only my first day. I've moved with my partner from Virginia back to Pennsylvania to work at another large, well-known university and should feel great, but I don't.

I pull some crystals out of my bag and arrange them on my desk. Discreet enough not to draw attention but powerful enough to help me feel better, I arrange my small pile of tumbled gemstones and place my favorites, the amethyst and fluorite, where I can see them. As the unproductive day draws to a close my supervisor wanders past and notices the rocks. *I know someone you should meet*, she says, pointing at the pile. I look at the name she's given me on a scrap of paper and feel a slight chill. Something feels right, for the first time all day. The massage therapist is her friend who owns a health center about twenty minutes away. I have very little cash to spare but feel inclined to call for an appointment, so I do.

Pulling up to the pretty house floods me with hope. I walk in the front door and am welcomed by a fluffy black cat bounding into a light and airy living space. When the therapist glides into the room, simultaneously extending her hand while shooing the kitty back into the private recesses of the home, she carries the subtle aroma of lavender and something else. I know now that it's sweetgrass that occupies every nook of the house and often lingers in my clothing when I leave. She and her home imbue me with a calm peacefulness, feelings I barely recognize.

For such a small woman, she's incredibly strong. The massage feels sure and connected in a way I've not before experienced, and there's something else about her too, something beyond the mechanics of the massage, though I'm not sure what. After she finishes, as I slowly pull myself back from a hazy reverie, I nearly drop my water when she begins speaking. In the midst of small talk about the weather, traffic, and my stiff neck, she blows my mind.

"Why do I keep getting the feeling *sister, sister* around you? Do you happen to know what that is?" Her cat eyes already seem to know the answer, but she levels her gaze in a way that makes me feel I should say something. I swallow hard to keep from crying and inspect my glass of water until I can talk without my voice shaking. Bursting into tears would be ridiculous. I don't even know this woman.

"That's probably my sister. She watches over me." My mom and I always maintained a strong spiritual connection to my sister, Denise, after her death, and we also agreed to keep the whole thing to ourselves. This is too much. Was this woman seeing spirits around me?

"That's probably it. The feeling is very strong and you're being watched over." *I cannot believe I'm having this conversation.* "So, would you like to schedule another appointment?" I nod a dumb yes and leave quickly, flooded with relief, sniffling back tears, and floating all at once.

Six months pass and while the massages have helped me begin to reclaim a painfully eroded sense of self, life still feels terrible. I can't quite shake the pain I've left behind in Virginia. Juggling one full-time job at an unstable, dysfunctional company while teaching part-time and defending myself against the politics of higher education had exhausted me. After watching my partner make a successful move to Pennsylvania, I had worked, interviewed, and waited almost a year until I found a job that would let me cover my bills and join him. I did a great job moving, managing my panic, facing the transition, and meeting the changes with spirit and hope. But despite all this, six months into my new job, I still feel terrifically disappointed in everything, especially myself.

I could be enjoying my new colleagues, new college town, new environment, new apartment, but rather than create what I desperately need—a space in my head where I can refocus, define my career goals, maybe let in some love and light—I drown in self-pity and petty politics. I find myself surrounded by some wonderful, but many indifferent, academics who generate lots of drama and little work. This lack of professionalism galls me. Money matters create mountains of stress and take up a lot of energy. My partner and I fight constantly, wondering if we should just end our relationship. I've been desperate, poor, and sad before, but I'm older now and the despair feels worse. I plod forward through my days with a heavy and obvious disappointment. Getting up in the morning becomes a challenge. I'm losing myself.

I've been a massage client for almost seven months when a flyer advertising a Reiki class snaps at me like a kite in strong wind. Unfamiliar with Reiki and without any money to spare, I still sense—I *know*—that I must be a part of this and sign up. Then the worrying begins… What have I just paid for? Who else will be in class? How weird is this going to be? I hope, in the deepest and most visceral way, that this class will help me find peace. I presume that other students will probably take this class to find "peace" in those prefabricated, new-agey ways. Not me. I want quantifiable results: better finances, a kinder, gentler relationship, and to stop loathing myself so damn much, but this all seems like much more than I can ever have. Still though, somewhere small and buried, in a place I can barely recognize, behind the tears and beyond the despair, I have a sudden and bizarre realization—I have *hope*.

We've all faced a moment (or even years' worth of moments) when we've felt the sinking, dark despair of knowing that whatever pains us—a situation, a relationship, a dream, our hearts—will probably never be right, pain-free, or okay. That life as we want it might not be ours. And this is okay. A "letting go" of these desperate expectations can be freeing and refreshing, much more so than grasping and controlling that which refuses to come under our power. Finding hope and letting it flower helps the negativity sting less and maybe even fade a bit. Hope encourages us to anticipate that which we may not see or think possible, and this allows us to build potential around outcomes. *And potential is where we store all of our personal power.*

Though it sounds a bit like feel-good rhetoric, recognizing and acknowledging more hopeful, positive ways of thinking about a situation or experience can actually change both the vibration surrounding and our reality of that experience! Simply, aligning ourselves with a kinder and more hopeful way of living and being feels good. Never underestimate the power of positive thought.

When I began writing, I had high hopes for grand success. I was hopeful, motivated, and determined. My very first submission consisted of an essay detailing why my kitten held such significance in my life. I sent in my essay — one painstakingly handwritten page — and the requested photo of my kitty, Nöel, and me. I talked about Nöel's place in my life, how this kitten had been a gift from my sister who had recently died tragically, and how he held incredible importance for me as the last link to an amazing woman I would never see again. I wrote with passion, vulnerability, and hope. My authentic self spoke up so loudly after being hidden for so long I almost didn't recognize her. I was proud of my writing, my courage, and my ability to splay my heart for some stranger to judge, all for $25 and a case of cat food.

No small feat for a twelve-year-old living in a house full of crazy rage.

After sending in the submission, I waited, and then I waited some more. Ironically, this provided fantastic practice for the writer I would become, the grown woman who would continue to wait, and then wait some more, except from agents and publishers instead of cat food company execs. The cat food company never responded to my heartfelt essay and, while I wondered with a sense of sadness which they hated more, the essay or the picture of chubby me in huge glasses, a flame of hope for myself and my story continued to burn.

Sometimes that little thread of hope helped me move outside the emotional pain of our broken home and actually function, while other times it reminded me that life wouldn't always be so ugly and hurtful, that circumstances would eventually shift one day. A recent encounter at the grocery store actually reminded me of that sweet first essay about Nöel and Denise. Although not a huge fan of the exact wording, I appreciated the spirit of the tattoo scrolled across my

grocery clerk's arm in too-fancy script: "Don't let the world beat you down when you can fight back." *Indeed*.

Excited and nervous and seven long months into my new job, I sit in my first Reiki class and struggle with the material, with the idea of a spiritually-guided life force energy that constantly flows within us. How can this be? How can I feel so lost and so deflated every day when some "power of the universe" is supposedly flowing through me? Academically it sort of makes sense, but spiritually I don't quite get it. This makes the agitation at spending money I don't really have to be in the class sting even worse.

Our teacher, my massage therapist, explains that Reiki channels the highest and purest energy already running through our systems in a way that completely bypasses our minds. In turn, we channel this energy by laying our hands in different positions and patterns on whoever needs healing.

This all seems remarkable to me, a worrier who constantly frets, sulks, and obsesses. Healing? With hands? The idea of being a channel for something greater, stronger, and more clear has a certain appeal I want to trust badly. I finally begin to feel less skeptical as I learn about things I've always suspected, like the body's ability to create its own illness.

Class proceeds peacefully until it's finally my turn to lie down on the table. As I look up at my classmates all around me, I'm shocked by ragged sobs. A classmate holding her hands at my feet for only a few moments has begun sobbing uncontrollably. Fear creeps up my spine as I hear her gasping. Suddenly, inexplicably, everyone in the room is crying and looking at me, bewildered.

Our Reiki master gathers everyone around me where I sit bundled inside a huge purple comforter, shaking. *We've experienced tremendous release here today* she explains, calming my sniffling classmate and assuring me I haven't done anything wrong. *Has this made anyone frightened of Reiki?* she asks. Every hand goes up around the circle, including mine. She nods and patiently explains how healing energy, always present and in motion, will often prompt dramatic "releases" or healings. We sit in wonder as she shares how those who work with Reiki might scream, cry, laugh, cough or do just about anything, all in response to an amazing and powerful healing taking place.

I mull over these possibilities in the subsequent weeks, much of which I spend quelling debilitating panic attacks I had successfully kept under control for almost ten years. The devastating attacks leave me feeling sad, disheartened, and flummoxed; I can't reconcile how attending a healing session has somehow broken me. Unable to function, I seek out my massage therapist. She provides a powerful and calming Reiki session to balance me and then shares something I can hardly believe: that I am experiencing a huge "healing crisis," the first courageous and inevitable step to deep and profound healing. I appreciate the information, but I just want to stop vomiting. And eventually, thankfully, I do. Once the panic attacks run their nasty, debilitating course, they never return.

When I recall that first day of Reiki training and the horrible weeks that followed as I desperately fought against a slow, steady slide into panic-induced insanity, I understand that without faith, hope, and determination, the illness would have taken me. Terrified that a prescription would dull and eventually snuff out my sometimes temperamental, often impatient, always passionate personality, I refused meds and doggedly worked my way through the horrid and often unbearable panic with Reiki, reflexology, massages, prayer, and hope.

That burgeoning hope, my ability to see past the pain, empowered me. Even when I could barely get out of bed, when even thinking about an attack would disable me, I knew my potential waited patiently for me, that laying my hands on strangers in comforting and caring ways for the first time in that class had opened up my heart and changed my quality of life, even if I couldn't see it yet. After the horror of my healing crisis, I saw signs, symbols, and messages everywhere, even in unimaginable ways and places and, finally, began to pay attention.

Barring ourselves from hope and claiming we can never do it, won't ever figure things out, will always fail, only brings us closer to self-defeat. These

That burgeoning *hope,* MY ABILITY to see past the *pain,* EMPOWERED *me.*

stories may or may not be true, but in the telling, we create the reality and help to cement our inevitable failure. A well-known motivational speaker suggests that when we hold unfulfilled dreams and hopes, when we *really* want something but aren't convinced we can own that thing, reach that goal, or achieve that dream, we should lean into it[1]. Good things, like success, can and do happen when we "lean into" our desires and pursue them fully with hope and determination, even when we don't already have the signed contract, the promise, or the guarantee. Leaning into hope—whether purposefully choosing to be positive when acting negatively would be easier or changing reality by changing belief—allows us to build momentum, rev up potential, and open up the realm of possibility.

Even when we can't see the whole path or the best way—common roadblocks when we try new things, take risks, or dare to hope for something we never thought we'd have—giving ourselves permission to let hope blossom and flow creates opportunity, movement, and potential. Find your faith, feel your hope, choose what seems like the most natural next stage to your journey, and let go!

I recently read an article in which the author declares hope problematic, something that turns us from our faith, for if we had "true" faith we wouldn't need hope's promises to sustain us. Accordingly, if we believe unconditionally in faith's promises, hope has no place and we have no need of it. *No need of hope?* Even Hildegard of Bingen, a 12th century writer and Benedictine abbess, knew the veracity of hope, claiming that "hope fights despair [as] the power of God within us that makes the impossible possible."[2] How can hope flowering in our hearts be anything but beautiful?

Buddhists cherish the concept that reality and our perception of reality are exactly the same; subsequently, when we fail to cultivate hope, we also refuse potential, making it impossible for possibility and opportunity to flourish, ultimately ignoring important information about ourselves.

Scary pitfalls like shadows, darkness, and the unknown are the very same things that force us to assume the best, step forward, and feel our way. Even when we can't see ahead, when we're unable to predict if the marriage will last, if the job will fulfill us, if our lives will give back what we have invested, we still inherently know we must allow ourselves to take a risk. Hoping opens us to healing, and healing nearly always involves movement and potential—two concepts that can intertwine in the most fantastic and beautiful of ways. Like a magnet that attracts wonderful new experiences and adventures, hope entices us. Go ahead… jump before you look, steer by moonlight, turn a fall into a dive. *Believe.*

Sea Glass Meditation

We've all been tumbled and tossed in our lifetimes, burying our pain where it won't show, sliding in and out of the ocean's ebb and flow as best we can with what we have. And as we negotiate the oceanscape of life, loss, and heartache, we realize that we have to emerge eventually, because life is waiting. And so we do. We re-emerge from the churning surf beautiful, transformed, different but the same, precious. Let hope blossom and flourish in your heart, and from that tiny spark, fan the flame. Watch it grow. Change your own reality.

Set Your Intention

Find a quiet space, sit alone, and take a deep breath. Close your eyes and think about what you want most from your life right at this moment. What would make you smile and feel full, whole, and satisfied that all is as it should be? Envision this desire, whatever it may be—wellness, love, financial freedom, peace—as completely as you can. Try to see it, feel it, sense how this satisfaction would fulfill you. Remember this feeling, for this is hope and, with purposeful determination, can help you create what you desire. Now set your intention using positive language:

I can have what I desire.

I understand my needs.

I feel hope.

Let the feeling grow and expand, and know that if you can see it, feel it, imagine it with purpose, *you can have it*.

Breathe the Reiki Energy

Slowly rub your hands together until you generate a slight heat between your palms. Once they have heated up, gently place your hands over your eyes. Breathe slowly and deeply, feeling each breath move into and out of your lungs. Imagine a glowing ball of indigo blue light on your forehead, between your eyes above the eyebrows. This light glows with a soft radiance that you breath in slowly. As you repeat your intentions to yourself, feel this indigo light filling you up, wrapping around each intention, and soaking into your thoughts. You feel complete joy, as though all the things you hope for and desire have already manifested. Lower your hands to your heart. Say the following with me:

All the power of the universe is here with me now.

A new reality can be yours.

Acknowledge Your Message

You walk along a calm beach in the early morning sun. You feel comfortable and safely enveloped in the early morning's warm sun just beginning to rise. The tide drifts out lazily, leaving rivulets of foam and bits of shell at your feet. Off to the side, you notice a small pod of dolphins gliding through the peaks of glossy waves far out at sea, creating a beautiful snapshot of light, life, and hope against the backdrop of a cloudless, blue sky. Life in this moment is rich, full, and complete.

As you walk slowly and gently along the shoreline, you look down and notice a shimmer in the damp sand. A rough and tumbled fragment of softly colored glass sits nestled amongst shells and rocks. The softly shaped glass is cool in your hand, its deep green reflecting gently. You take a few more steps, this time towards a small tidal pool that has gathered at a low point near the tide line. Here you find a gently curved piece of chocolate brown glass glistening next to tiny sand crabs oblivious to its beauty.

As the sun climbs higher, you find more forgotten treasures—a soft square of seafoam green, smooth like a worry stone between thumb and forefinger; a sliver of brown, tiny and perfect for slipping into your pocket; the thick lip of a green beer bottle turned precious and pretty; and a stunning slab of soft white, its thick and frosted edges rubbed silky from years of tumbling in the surf.

You place your footfalls carefully as the tide continues to release more of its bounty… bits of conch and scallop, mermaid's purses and flotsam, quartz and seaweed. One rogue wave defies the tide, washes gently over your unsuspecting feet, and deposits a beautiful and rare piece of blue glass in the damp and curling sand by your toes. The thick glass glows a deep indigo in the sun. Its pointy shape, reminiscent of a crystal point, feels perfect for writing in the sand. The rare treasure is even more precious in your hands. The sea glass, gifted to you from the sea, carries a message. You bend to the sand and the glass moves in your hand across the crusty surface of sand, leaving words in its wake.

What does the message say? How does it express hope? Help? Healing?

You straighten and tilt your face to the sun, knowing the message is yours, understanding that it holds the key to your potential. You look at the various pieces of sea glass in your hand—bottle green to chocolate brown, smoky white to indigo blue—thank them for their help, and lay them gently down in the sand where their kaleidoscopic reflection reminds you that rainbows come in all sizes.

Sit quietly and take a deep breath, feeling the peace and joy of the moment. You have left the glass behind, but its energy remains.

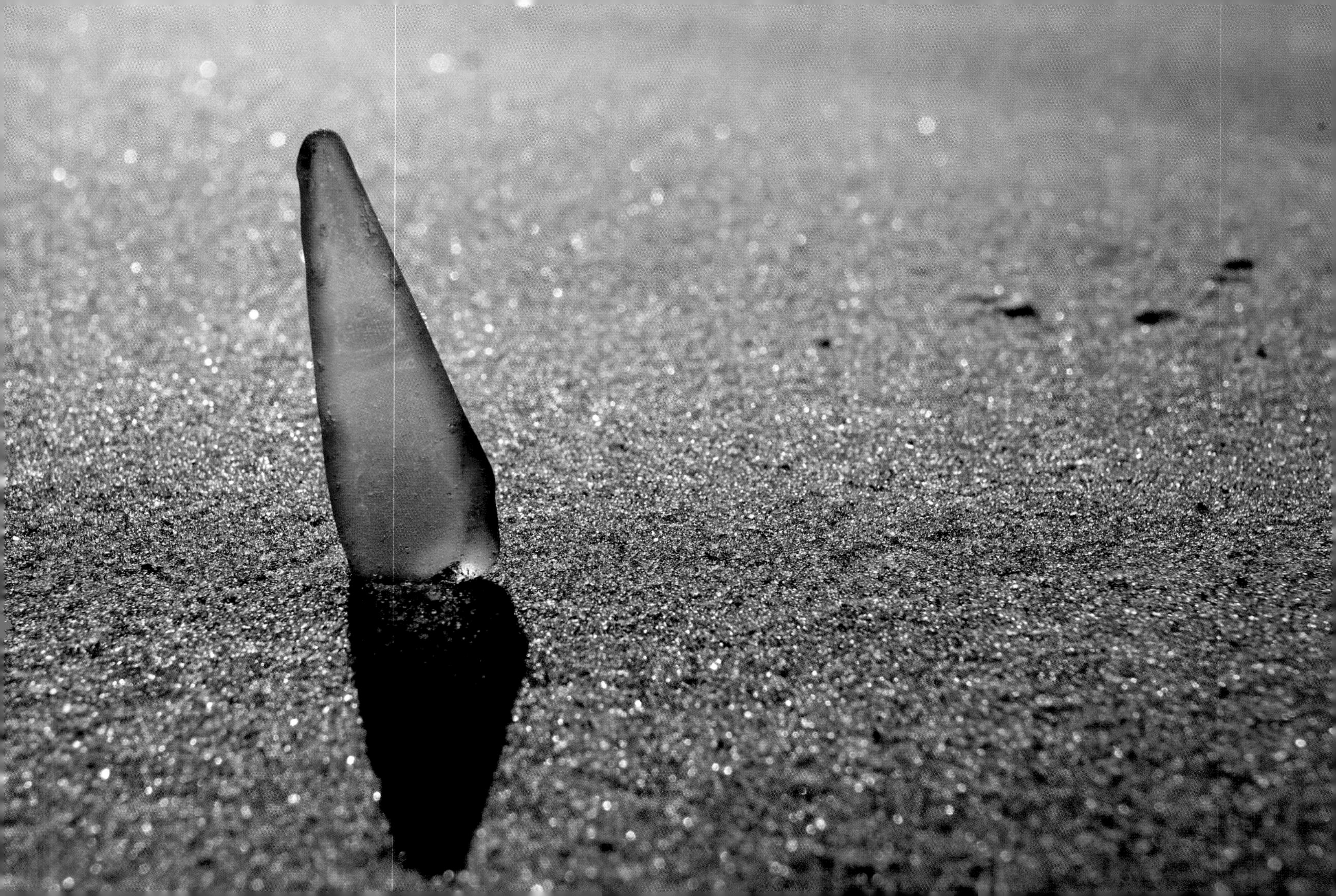

Sea Glass Exercise

The sea sent a message of hope for you. Do you feel its inherent power and spirit? Whether you feel inspired or nervous, skeptical or willing, take a moment to write it down in a private place. Remember that we often resist hope when we feel battered and beaten, churned and tossed, but potential waits for you to remember who you are, how great are your capabilities, and how much you are truly worth.

Sit quietly and think of all the pieces of your life that make you feel satisfied. In what parts of your life are you good or gifted? What kinds of tasks can you comfortably take on? Maybe your life reflects socially-noteworthy successes, like being a great mom, a successful businessperson, or a gifted artist. Or perhaps you consider your achievements more modest, like having a nice smile, being a good driver, or being capable of making a great breakfast. Whatever your skills, consider these things without judgment and appreciate yourself. How do you feel when you think about these kind and gifted parts of yourself with appreciation?

Keeping these positive feelings in mind, on a blank sheet of paper list circumstances, people, or situations in your life that you find negative, challenging, hopeless, or saddening. Be honest and open because only you will ever see this list. How do you feel making this list? Does it seem long or overwhelming? Are you judging yourself for having so many unresolved moments in your life?

Starting right now, with the first item at the top of the list, write down one way of *thinking* about this situation that would bring you peace of mind. Even if this thought doesn't necessarily solve the issue at this moment, write down a way you can think about it more positively. Although you may not immediately feel positive, try it anyway.

For example, perhaps you have unfriendly, loud, or rude neighbors whom you do not like. This exercise could involve something as simple as deciding that their rude behavior will no longer have the power to upset you. Instead of letting their behavior fan your flame of resentment and hurt, you now choose to turn off your normal frustrated response and let go of the situation.

How does this feel? You haven't "fixed" anything except your own response and perception of the situation, but if you persist in this exercise, *the shift in your perception will begin to shift reality*.

Each day, at a time when you have a few minutes to spare for yourself, take out your list and consider the next item. Think about one simple way of choosing to think differently about the challenge or frustration, and then try it. State this shift out loud. Rather than thinking, "I don't like the way so-and-so ignored me when I was out back, watering the flowers. She should have at least said hello and acknowledged me," state: "I love and enjoy the beauty and safety of my home. I'm so happy I have been able to garden and decorate it in ways that leave me feel happy and satisfied." Who really knows if your neighbor will ever invite you over, say a few kind words, or acknowledge

Bits & Baubles

My favorite piece of sea glass, unimpressive at first glance, is apparently a treasure. Only one inch long, the little shard is only a tiny bit thicker than a pencil and shifts from a cornflower blue on one end to a clear white on the other. One side shows embossing from what was likely once the bottom of an old bottle. According to collectors, its color makes it a 1/600 find and, ironically, I can't even remember how it came to me. All of my other sea glass finds—common but beautiful greens, browns, and whites—come from the beautiful beaches of Cape May, New Jersey. How ironic and befitting that the most rare piece comes from who-knows-where, possibly a tagalong in a box of tumbled rocks I once bought. I always enjoy finding these little bits of frosty color while walking the foamy tide, and I appreciate their lesson: giving focus to the small and unimpressive in our lives can bring us grand discovery. If you're lucky enough to find a piece of sea glass, take an appreciative look at what was probably once a discarded beer bottle and consider…how often do we have the opportunity to hold transformation in our own hands and don't even realize it?

you but, much more importantly, the maddening feelings of unfairness will fade since reprogramming your thinking shifts focus to that over which you *do* have control.

Once you have covered every challenge in your list once, go back and add a second way of feeling positive (again, whether you actually feel this way or not yet) about this situation or person. Eventually you will begin to check things off this list, not necessarily because situations have resolved as you might have guessed— the neighbors probably haven't moved away—but your perceptions have! And when perception shifts to the positive, reality follows.

Shifting the vibration around a situation *changes the situation itself*, and in this way you live the sea glass cycle. Your improved outlook converts trash to treasure by revising limiting beliefs into a new, positive light that no one controls but you. Turning hope's potential into a beautiful new reality isn't just for alchemists or magicians—this power truly is yours.

Sea Glass Affirmation

~My heart knows the journey.

Transformed by wind, air, earth, and fire,

Discarded, it tumbles and tosses.

I emerge whole, transformed, real.

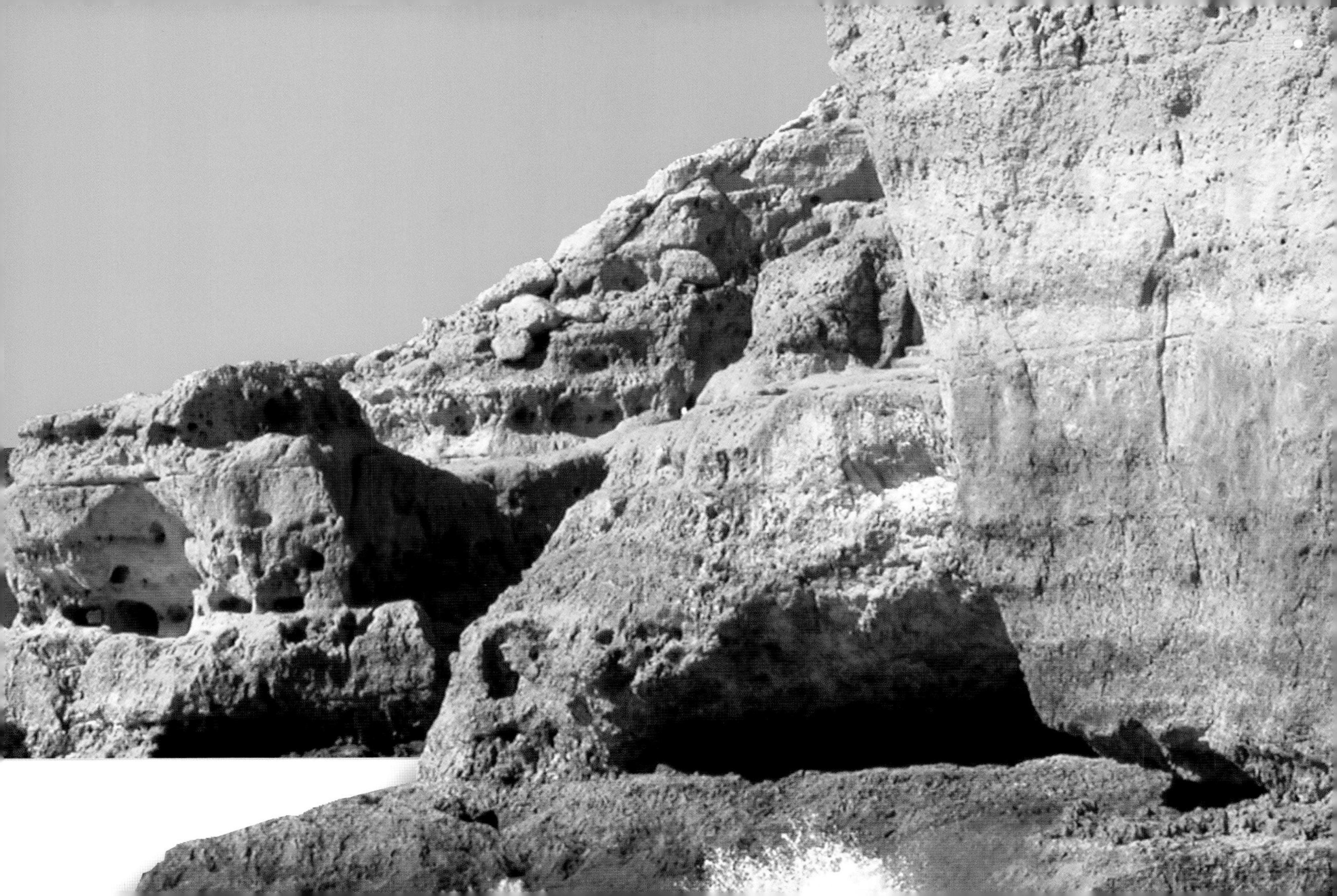

Accepting
Surrender

Each time we step on a beach, trillions of sand grains surrender to us, accommodating our weight and space. Lost to our comprehension are the infinite years spent tumbling and crashing to make these grains of sand possible. How many times in our lives are we challenged to surrender ourselves to a greater plan or process? And how often do we resist? A wealth of information lies available to us in that space, that interstice, between surrender and grasp. When we overtly and obsessively attach ourselves to goals and outcomes, forgetting the necessity of the journey, we lose the knowledge that comes with "being here now." Letting go—surrendering—brings us closer to a deeper understanding of the patterns of life. Surrendering brings us closer to grace.

I dance around my office, stopping occasionally to reread the email. I have sold an essay to one of the best known anthologies on the market. I'll be getting $150 and, even more valuable, a byline. While I don't ignore the money—that much cash equals almost 15 hours of part-time work tutoring students online—I also know it'll be gone in a flash with one or two fill-ups and a trip to the grocery. In a world where authors vie for publication along with hundreds of thousands of other aspiring writers, a byline is golden, and of course I want my name attached to a commercially successful series. I've published before, in other anthologies and also academic publications, but this acceptance rocks my world. I read the email yet again—my essay has earned a spot from over two thousand entries in a new *Chicken Soup for the Soul*® anthology. Unbelievable!

I sit back down to write an email to my friend's mother to get her permission to publish since her son, my friend's brother, features in the essay. This isn't my family's story and to publish it without her knowing feels wrong. I begin a happy, somewhat stunned email sharing my elation, nervousness, and exceptional good fortune at scoring such a publication spot for the essay, and I thank her for the opportunity to tell her son's once-silent story. I finish by requesting written permission to progress with the publisher.

The following afternoon I open her reply email and my stomach knots. Suddenly scared for her son, for all his years of struggle and hurt, she hesitates to sign the release allowing the essay to appear. She wishes, she writes, to keep her son safe from ridicule and harm. Although no family names appear in the essay, she worries he will feel a backlash, an unknown ramification of telling his story, of sharing the joy he found in his grandma's presence. I read the email and try not to cry. I am utterly flummoxed. Her love shines in an undeniable and unmistakable way. What can I say to a mom wanting to protect her autistic adult son?

And that, I think with a sinking heart, *is the end of that.*

I mull this turn of events while driving to a Reiki session that evening; I look forward to this as, on this evening, I am client rather than practitioner. As I pull onto Route 45 and begin the last leg of my drive, I experience an amazing epiphany. *Let it go.* I feel this in an almost palpable way. *Let it go.* Something deep inside me cracks open, letting love and light pour in. I see a mother wishing more for her son, hoping he will successfully negotiate the world without her one day, showering him with what she has to give—love and protection.

I lie comfortably on the massage table, close my eyes, and almost instantly I see the story rolling through my head. I know the difficult life this autistic child has lived. I know him, feel him, sense pain and confusion. With each pass of my therapist's hands over me, I know the story will be published…or it won't. Somehow, I feel that regardless of the outcome, the Universe insures that this disappointment will be just fine. A fairly intense worrywart, I glow with the unusual knowledge, sitting up at the end of my session smiling and lighthearted.

The calmness, the peacefulness all feels very unfamiliar to me, and I struggle to name it. What is this feeling? I know I have surrendered something—some kind of anxiety attached to the outcome—and enjoy the unfamiliar delight.

The next day, I'm surprised but pleased to see a follow-up email from my friend's mom. I had written back, acknowledging her wishes for her son and his story, and assuring her that I would do whatever she requested, even if it meant declining publication. I also explained that the story was always and foremost meant as a gift to those who read it, to let others with grown autistic children read about one young man who created a special, heartwarming bond with his grandma. I always believed that the beauty of his story comes from his trust and surrender to a woman who loved him completely and unconditionally.

My friend's mom says I touched her heart. She muses (to my horror) that she is perhaps "being tricked" somehow by the beautiful words I have written in my email, and in the end agrees that the story should be published with the hope it will provide support to other families with grown autistic children. In short, I have her blessing.

I sit in front of the email and feel it again, the letting go, the surrender that had imbued me the night before. The letting go — the "letting Reiki" — had opened up an energetic pathway where none stood before. I promise to remember this feeling, this *just let go* whisper. The feeling is nothing short of throwing the door wide and inviting in hope. *What is intended for you will return to you.* The lesson continually finds me, even on those days I rather it wouldn't, when I prefer to spin inside hopeless worry, something I know well.

We all experience moments — sometimes even lifetimes — when we fall back into old habits comprised of worry, panic, and frustration. Because so few of us learn as children how to deal with difficult emotions in positive, healthy ways, we often fail at self-support and comfort as adults. During times of distress we gasp and struggle to stay afloat while inflating our expectation of a perfect (and, thus, impossible) outcome. This leads us to grasp blindly and wildly for the best solutions to what we perceive as unsolvable situations.

Consider, though, how often the seeds of self-realization are truly sown by loss of control and surprise.[1] Since we barely recognize this perspective, it's not surprising we struggle to embrace it consciously. Losing control in Western culture represents a loss of all that's decent: self, sanity, logic, reason, worth. We take pride in presenting ourselves as a culture of obvious resistance and strength, adept at either dodging or subverting that which makes us uncomfortable; staying "in control" at all times sits high on our list of acceptable behaviors.

Diving into our life's greatest challenges by conversely letting them go allows us to unearth the "secret face" of our most difficult experiences by providing a pathway by which we discover we are infinitely more capable than we imagine. We don't usually consider how we find courage and strength when dealing with uncomfortable challenges; we either face the situation and wrangle our way through it as best we can or, if we're lucky, hand it over to someone else. How, though, might we face challenges without the fight?

Simply, the pathway is surrender. Lama Surya Das tells us that "the art and practice of freedom [is] the practice of letting go," attained through breathing and meditation…but what about those moments when we don't want to breathe deeply and meditate? What of those days when rage, frustration, and fear overwhelm us and leave us gasping? Shouldn't we be armoring ourselves against vulnerability?

The answer remains the same: let go. This ability takes practice and courage, especially in a culture where the concept of using nonaction—essentially doing nothing very consciously—to defuse a situation looming impossibly huge and foreign seems laughable. Much more used to grasping and grabbing, tugging and forcing, we must cultivate the art of letting go through patience, time, and determination. Sometimes, surrender actually seems too intuitive, too easy; in those moments we sadly tend to discount it and shrug away its value. Try recognizing those moments in your life, gauging when you feel most positive, even when you can't change or fix a situation, and when you are left feeling powerless. You may be surprised to find that surrender, in whatever form it takes, creates amazing clarity around challenges.

Last year my partner and I went through the trials of socializing a feral kitten. I desperately wanted to adopt the little guy, but since I had no idea what I was doing, I spent a lot of time Googling "feral kitten" and following my instincts. I spent every evening outside encouraging him to eat, helping him get used to human company, and using Reiki to ease his transition into trust.

One day, concerned that the kitten would be outside during upcoming bad weather, my young neighbor decided to catch him. I watched in horror from the window as she rushed up to my porch with her dogs, calling for the kitten. Intent and curious, the dogs strained on their leashes and barked ferociously as my neighbor juggled her cell phone, the two leashes, a lit cigarette, and had a conversation, all at top volume. Busy with her cigarette and yelling loudly, at both the dogs and into the phone, she missed the kitten's mad dash at escape.

"Where'd it go?!" she screamed into the phone. "Crap! It disappeared!"

Of course he did, was my ungracious thought. The kitten was terrified, hunkering under a bush, I was livid, and she was clueless. All I could think was, "WHY are you undoing all of my hard work?" Then I caught myself, took a breath, and realized she wanted to save the kitten too, not scare it on purpose. If he was meant to live in her home, he would. It really was that simple! The situation concerned the kitten's welfare, not my ego bruised by her "undoing" of my work. Of course, nothing had actually been "undone." I had told myself that story out of frustration, anger, and fear.

A few weeks later, the kitten decided on his own that he would like to test drive coming inside our home, and then moved in for good. We recently celebrated his three year anniversary of venturing inside; these days, he plunks down for head rubs when once he ran in terror. When I look at him, I see a miracle, the purest result of letting go.

Martha Beck calls it "joyful detachment"—letting things unfold as they will, trusting that the Universe (or God, or Buddha, or Allah, or whomever) creates the highest and best outcome for the situation, *whatever it may look like*. A hard concept to remember sometimes, but a really phenomenal one as well. I could have demanded the right to publish the story from my friend's mom, making her feel small, foolish, and uneducated in the face of my big accomplishment. I could have used her unfamiliarity with the publishing industry to make demands of her, twist the truth, squeeze the permission from her. Or I could have moved forward with her son's story without telling her anything at all. How often do we take these kinds of enraged power stances, insisting on and pushing our agendas with the belief that our brute strength will create the outcome we want and deserve?

Really surrendering and letting go doesn't mean leaving life to chance, or stopping participation in those things you find important and rewarding. Of course I wrote back to my friend's mother and quietly explained my intention with the essay; my challenge and blessing came with consciously *letting go of the outcome* rather than wheedling, pushing, or demanding.

Consciously letting go is an active choice, difficult enough for the average person, but one absolutely fraught with peril for those of us who have grown up hypervigilant of the next trauma or personal disaster. In some cases, surrender actually feels akin to death since we have grown to believe that safety/success/ acceptance only comes from carefully controlling a situation. Conversely, letting go involves losing dependency on the external structures — the media, family rules of engagement, learned behaviors — that have always supplied our cues, and relying upon a guidance system that comes from within.[2]

As we begin to question our need to hold and control, we slowly understand that our mapping and planning, while important, are more tentative than we realize. We all desire some form of happiness and our egos tell us we deserve to have these wants met. I worked hard writing that essay and socializing that kitten — why *shouldn't* both successes be mine? They would in time, but consider that "successful" outcomes don't always look as we imagine them.

In Reiki, we encourage and practice the unfamiliar by surrendering our wants and desires to the highest and greatest healing. Rather than asking for this person, this animal, this thing to be healed, get better, and come back to us whole and well, we instead are challenged to ask for the situation and the outcome to reflect the highest and greatest purpose, *whatever that may look like*, and something we may not recognize from our limited human perspective. This kind of challenging thinking moves our egos aside so healing can happen.

Because most of our mental suffering comes from the tightness with which we hold our beliefs,[3] the idea of letting go and surrendering may at first feel like a flimsy barrel ride over treacherous falls, especially when an outcome doesn't meet our expectation. In the end, though, what exactly do we achieve with worry and fret? You know the answer. While surrender may seem like it opens our most vulnerable spaces, it actually does the hardest and best work of cracking open our fabricated shells, allowing us to be free and more whole, helping us to move towards grace.

Letting go to surrender involves making a deep and conscious commitment…to yourself! Trust yourself to know the best path, to drop worry, to feel calm and able. You already hold this ability. Just like walking along the sand, let go, "let Reiki," and enjoy the freedom that comes with knowing your needs are met.

Set Your Intention

Sit alone quietly. Take a moment for yourself to think about your life and the way you keep your world in order. We all tend to hold onto things, people, and expectations, though some of us grasp more tightly than others. Where do you hold too tightly? Is there something or someone in your world that feels overpowering or out of control?

What would happen if you let go? Set your intention using positive language:

I consciously surrender to _____
(fill in the blank)

I let go of my need to _____
(fill in the blank)

I release control of _____
(fill in the blank)

Remember to state your intention in the positive, allow yourself to let go, believe.

Breathe the Reiki Energy

Close your eyes and relax into a comfortable position. Put your hands on your stomach and breathe evenly and deeply, feeling your belly rise and fall with each breath. Don't worry if your thoughts feel distracting and zig-zaggy; let these thoughts grab for your attention, and then let them pass by.

As you breathe more and more deeply, calming your mind, begin scanning your body. Start at your head and move down slowly, noticing where you hold tightness or strain, pain or discomfort. When you find a place that feels "stuck," breathe into that place by envisioning a deep purple light filling the area and melting whatever pain or holding you feel. Keep breathing deeply throughout this exercise until you have reached your toes. Scan your body again and keep breathing into any tightness or discomfort until you feel relaxed.

Move both hands from your abdomen to your heart, breathing slowly and deeply. Repeat your intention to yourself with belief that it is true, and say the following with me:

All the power of the universe is here with me now.

Your message seeks you.

A light breeze plays across your face as you visualize yourself about to step onto a beautiful beach. This may be a favorite place you have visited many times before, a place from your daydreams, or even someplace you have seen only in pictures. Know that your visit to this place will bring tremendous joy. Crystal blue light slides in and out from behind huge clouds as you walk across delicate grains of sand towards the ocean. Each time you step forward, the sand shifts, gives way, and holds you like a steadying hand. In this moment, with the sand holding every step, you understand how you have been supported many times in your life.

You near the ocean and, although the waves roar loudly in the sea, they hold no fear for you. You slide into the warm water, and delight in the way it swirls slowly around your ankles, knees, thighs, stomach, and finally shoulders as you continue to step forward into the unknown.

Looking skyward into the blue, you surrender; you lift your feet, lie back, and float, fully supported by the water, wind, and sky. If fear nibbles around the edges of your mind, visualize yourself as a white, weightless being with a light that glows from within. This light protects you at all times, allowing you to bob and float on waves without fear. You are supported and protected fully. Floating feels glorious and free.

You effortlessly bob on the waves, the warm water moving you gently. You float like this for as long as feels comfortable.

Eventually, when you are ready to touch land again, the water effortlessly bobs you back to the shore. You lower your legs and breath in the sky one last time. Waves slowly fall away from your shoulders, stomach, thighs, and knees as you move towards the beach. You lower your gaze when the waves are no higher than your ankles and see marks in the sand, perhaps writing. Joy fills your heart; the sands holds a message just for you. You step from the water slowly. *What do you see? Symbols? Words? Is the message hard to acknowledge? A new treasure? Look at the sand now, and accept this message sea and sand has left for you…*

When you have finished working with your message, drag your foot gently across the sand, erasing it from physical existence while locking it into your own memory. Thank the sand for its gift, and notice the way each grain holds you as you stand, always surrendering to your body but remaining strong. Come back to the present and continue to stay quiet for a moment. Give silent thanks.

Sand Exercise

What message did the sand have for you? Was it easy to hear? Hard to digest? Without judgment or fear, take a moment to write it down in a safe and private place.

Think of a time when you were supported unconditionally. This could have been a brief blink in time or an event that lasted months or years. What were the hallmarks of this support? Did you ask for it or did it come naturally? What made this support memorable? Consider that we all experience support in our own unique ways; perhaps your support came from a person, place, or animal. Think about what it would be like to provide this kind of support to yourself, unconditionally, always.

Write down one thing—a hope, a dream, a task, an errand—in which you need support and encouragement. How hard is this thing you need to do? What makes it so hard? Next to this task, write down, "I surrender [this task] for the highest and greatest good. I am divinely supported and protected." Say this affirmation daily, with confidence and a full heart.

Perhaps it will take you a few days or months to complete this task; perhaps it will take a lifetime. How long your task will take depends partly on its depth and complexity, and partly on letting go of your goal while moving towards it. Journal on this continuously, once or twice a week. Investigate honestly what it could feel like to let go completely of outcome and focus instead on the journey.

Repeat this again for another task, big or small, taking time to journal or jot notes about these experiences, noticing any changes in your ability to handle yourself in the midst of these situations. In what way has perspective changed? Soon you will come to understand and recognize those moments that are yours to shift and bend, and those that require quiet surrender.

Each time you face a challenge that looms:

- Assess your abilities honestly.

- Ask yourself where you stand and what you can affect.

- Picture the best case scenario.

- Do your very best, despite any fear or hesitation.

- Surrender.

Silt & Sand

Craggy and uneven, ugly and beautiful all at once, driftwood comes from all manner of places. Sitting in the sea for ages, once it hits the shore it might appear smooth, worn, lovely, or ragged. Driftwood holds a special, pure quality for me, and I know immediately if I should take it home when I've stumbled upon it. You too will know if a beach item would like to come home with you. If you are unsure, ask, and then follow the next feeling you get. Use driftwood the same way you would a crystal, placing it where it brings you peace or where it seems to want to go. If you don't have the luxury of being near a beach that regularly gifts its shores with driftwood, you might also enjoy working with crystals that heal the heart and root chakras. You might try rose quartz, aventurine, malachite, and rhodochrosite for your heart, and garnet, hematite, apache tear, bloodstone, and ruby for the root, as well as any others to which you are drawn. The possibility for healing using nature's gifts is endless.

Sand Affirmation

I walk lightly onto sand, supported and whole.   Reiki holds me as I release outcome and ego.
Stepping into the space between grasping and letting go,   I embrace surrender.

Cultivating Compassion

Just as starfish regenerate lost limbs by using an inherent ability to become whole again, we too hold the key to renewal and healing when we tend the place within ourselves where compassion flows. We have all experienced sadness and doubt, feeling the joy that comes with contentment and peace slip from us. The powerful stories we tell ourselves during the times when we have become lost to our soul's purpose often smack with self loathing, fear, and judgment. Compassion fades into a backdrop of anxiety and unrest. What might it feel like to release and refuse judgment, choosing instead to see ourselves and others with the compassion we hold in our hearts but have forgotten how to exercise?

I sidestep a truck making a tight turn and move closer to the shoulder of the road. Although I'm nervous about walking all the way from the salon to the mall where my mom works, I do it anyway because I feel like a shaggy dog and because life goes on. I've looked like a wreck at school for the past few months. My friends know I'm still in terrific pain over my sister's death and they have been patient and caring. I am spending the second half of 8th grade in a haze, sitting in silence during what used to be my strongest classes, ducking into the bathroom during change of class to chew the inside of my cheek and stop crying. Already shy, I have completely closed down.

One day in April, I realize just how bad I look. I have not taken care with myself beyond a basic shower for months and, at 12-years-old and struggling to blossom into young adulthood, I feel behind and out of synch, unable to speak the language of smart clothes and pretty looks. I need to clean up. For once in my life, I take a practical tact: Book reports are due Monday, one of the boys earns a detention, my sister has died, I need a haircut. Life goes on.

The very first time Rochele cut my hair, she was kinder than any stylist I had met. Since then I have followed her from salon to salon, her most current located on a hideously busy street that accommodates five lanes of traffic and draws business from the nearby mall where my mother works. We don't have a car, so I have taken the bus to the salon and, with my new haircut, am now walking to meet my mother at work where I'll curl up with a book for the balance of the afternoon until we take the bus home together at 5:30.

Squeaking along the highway, I hug the shoulder and try to stay away from traffic. I can't help swinging my head a little, feeling pleased and proud at the springy curls around my face. I even like the smell of the sticky-sweet hairspray. I feel…nice.

When Rochele first met me, she just kept laughing and shaking her head, wondering at all the curls still on my head when so much hair lay scattered on the floor. *You've got the most beautiful, thickest hair I've ever seen.* It took a few visits before I could finally relax. Having anyone touch my hair had always been physically painful, and most stylists brushed it too hard. Even though I felt stupid about being so sensitive, my head was always in terrible pain from the cruel, hard yanks. As a youngster, I often cried at the stress and pain. Stylists hate kids who cry.

Always embarrassed by the huffs and tsks coming from behind me as razor-sharp scissors clicked near my ears, not until I am older do I realize the root of this obvious irritation — those stylists wanted my thick curls on a customer who would have appreciated them, not a child who would never style them beyond a mop of frizz. At a tender 12-years-old, I finally see it too: Rich and lustrous hair completely wasted on a crying fat girl. *It's okay*, I reason, *I hate her too.*

I catch myself staring at the mirrored walls inside the mall entrance and am happy with the reflection. This is a first. I don't usually like mirrors. Winding my way past fast food stores, jewelry kiosks, and stores with cute, super-hip clothing that will never fit me, I find my mother in her department, folding lingerie.

Mom gives me her widest smile while telling me how pretty and grown up I look. She seems better today, more able to push her pain aside and less likely to crumble, something she usually reserves for evenings when the two of us are alone. With a wink and a wave, she turns to help a customer. She has to work for another two hours, so I settle into a back stockroom floor with my Judy Blume and a dismantled mannequin. There are worse ways to spend Saturday afternoon; I could be home, alone with my father.

Riding home on the bus, Mom and I talk. For a few minutes I forget where we're going, but then I notice Mom's eyes; remembering we're headed home, the dread creeps onto her face and her eyes cloud over. I hate this part, when we're nearly there. I secretly fantasize about living in the lingerie department where she works. The small department sits in a cozy upper-level corner of a local department store. It brims with bras, slips, housecoats, and nightgowns. Soft things. Nothing hard or sharp. Mom likes the quiet of the department, a place where she can bring order to her world by fixing a tag or straightening a hanger. I love the peace.

As the bus hits a rut, Mom and I bump into each other on the seat. She suggests some ucky things for dinner, leftovers I don't want, but I nod. I've already had Roy Rogers for lunch and a twenty-five dollar haircut. We need to save money and eat leftovers. The bus lurches again, nearing our stop. We always take the bus. Mom hasn't been able to get another car since her accident and the bus is cheap. We never borrow Dad's car, even to get groceries. Mom asked once and he went crazy. This seems stupid and unfair to me since, despite the impending divorce from my mother, a divorce he insisted upon, he eats the food we buy, lives in the house with us, and talks openly to his girlfriend— until recently one of my mother's close friends—on the phone daily. Even worse, I have to hear him chat sweetly about her cute and pretty granddaughter who is my age. As if I care.

I do. *My god, it hurts.*

After dinner, I bump into my father while carrying laundry to the washer. This happens sometimes. The laundry room sits right next to my father's domain, the den. I try to stay upstairs at night when my father is home, but I wanted to help with laundry as a thank you for the hair cut. I look up too late. My father stands in the dining room doorway, effectively blocking my way. I stand awkwardly by the kitchen sink, arms loaded with panties and bras. Wanting to move through the dining room. Past him. Wishing I had been quicker so I could have already slid into the tiny laundry room beyond.

"Your hair."

I nod once, quietly, slowly. Negotiating conversation with my father reminds me of what it must be like working with wild animals—no quick moves or sudden stops lest the animal strike. "I got it cut," I say carefully. *Don't say anything that will make him mad.* He looks me over, nods once, smiles. I approach with supreme caution.

"I got it cut? At this place? Near the mall?" All of my statements to my father rise at the end, like my sentences are really questions. Because, in reality, they are. This is me, asking permission to breathe, speak, be. He continues to smile and appraise my hair. I can't believe I'm doing this, talking to him as though everything is fine and peaceful, not broken or bent at all. Talking to him as though he can be trusted, *as though he likes me*.

"What do you think?" I scrunch up my nose, giving him permission not to like it, desperately wanting him to. He nods.

"It makes you look just like Denise." For a moment I lose my breath. This is very good news to me. I love the idea of looking like my beautiful older sister. Just as I feel my heart slow, as I begin to lower my shield of printed cotton panties to my side, he strikes. During the time it takes for him to blink once, he sees me. He looks down into my eyes and his expression transforms, like his face has been made of putty and someone has heated it to an unpleasant temperature. The stunned look makes me wonder if he has just now remembered he's talking to his youngest daughter. Talking to not-Denise. His eyes turn hard.

"I don't like it." He says it so casually, the dagger-words glance right off me at first. "Why are you trying to look like her?" I try not to double over from the emotional punch I feel in my stomach. "You should change it," he says with a final nod as he marches past me to the refrigerator.

I take my dirty clothes to the laundry room and shut the tiny door. I wait there, leaning against the washer, biting my lip, trying not to cry. Finally, I hear him go back into the den and pull the door. In a fury I shove my clothes, panties and bras in a jumble, into the washer, tears rolling down my face. In the pile is a camisole of Denise's made of beautiful peach satin. She had given it to me last year because she knew how much I loved it. I only ever wash the camisole by hand with extra-gentle soap in the old porcelain laundry sink, carefully laying it out to dry on a fresh towel. I've always loved it for its delicate color but now I wear it whenever I can, just to feel the silky softness of her memory against me.

Choking on my ragged breath and wiping the snot from my face, I shove the delicate camisole behind the washer. I jam it between the unpainted wall and back of the machine. I smash it deeper and deeper into the dirty tangle of cobwebs and dusty hoses until I can barely reach it and hear a telltale rip as the beautiful fabric catches and tears on a stray nail. *Who cares*, I think, *we all get torn apart eventually anyway*.

I feel such sadness for this 12-year-old me, for the young girl devastated by such blithe, easily tossed words that both cut her open and sealed her shut for so many years. But rather than loathe my father, I can now breathe, take a step back, and invite the little girl into my heart, easing her pain with the love, support, and kindness she desperately needed. The power in this, of rewriting her story and consequently healing both her and my grown self thirty years later, is tremendous.

Oftentimes, when our egos get in the way or when our own hurt or self-loathing overwhelm us, it feels much easier to act in ways for which we later feel shame and embarrassment. We've all done this at one time or another. We are human and, as such, we have all spread gossip, treated someone poorly, made or went along with a nasty joke at someone's expense. We have all hurt someone, in some way, even when we knew what we were doing.

While I make no excuses for my father's wretched behavior, neither can I completely condemn a man I barely know. I don't know how to throw a punch, but that doesn't mean I too haven't been culpable of forgetting the place where compassion resides. Yes, I have inflicted hurt. And I have grown to realize that *even the smallest acts of compassion can bring God into our hearts*. This alone is reason enough to rewrite those false, arbitrary, lying stories that strip us of self-love and confidence, that tell us we're nothing more than garbage.

Children and adults who have experienced trauma tend to create the worst, most pessimistic stories from which rise grossly judgmental and often inaccurate beliefs. These negative stories trump all other information and seduce us into believing tremendous lies about self-worth, family ties, life, and fate. When we tell ourselves that we're ugly, unable, stupid, powerless, fat, useless, and every other horrible thing we can imagine, *we believe every word*.

In those years when all I knew were screams and slammed doors and pain pouring through the walls, I inadvertently wove grand, scary, sad, and confusing stories around myself and my family, working out a rationale that, in retrospect, is understandable, especially given my age, but grossly flawed. **Unfortunately, I lived my stories as Truth.**

My dad is mean
because I am unlovable.

My mother is upset
because I am useless.

My friends date and I don't
because I am disgusting.

Because my stories relied on everyday experience, and my days so often brimmed over with family dysfunction and confusion, I failed to learn the most important and fundamental characteristic—that a story, at its core, is a *fabrication*.

My mother told similar stories. Each revolved around my father and focused on times when things were better, a point in time *before*—before the Korean war, my birth, this mysterious uncontrollable

rage, his affair. These tales include humor, compassion, and worst of all, incredible gentleness, something I have never experienced from this man. My mother used to recount the time my dad found a box of filthy abandoned kittens, eyes glued shut from a raging infection, which he then caringly, lovingly, and patiently tended every day, without help, until their little eyes cleared up and they could be adopted out. I wish I knew that man, and not the one who threatened me with a belt when I was afraid to take my cough medicine. This supremely confusing story of gentle compassion for helpless kittens is my mother's to hold and cherish, not mine, and that has to be okay.

Gandhi said, "The only devils in the world are those running around in our hearts. That is where the battle should be fought." Compassion flowing freely and unhaltingly to others comes from a healed heart. Only someone able to make peace with their own conflicts, embrace their own fears, acknowledge their own weakness, and open their hearts to themselves can truly show compassion to others. Compassion happens when we give of ourselves freely, not just when the mood strikes, we're feeling holiday guilt, or because we feel poorly about being a flawed human and doing anything helps to make us feel better.

Hildegard of Bingen, an exceptional medieval abbess, suggests that humankind enact compassion through seven divine laws. To modern eyes, these laws look a lot like suggestions for eco-conscious living, such as drinking fresh, untainted water (easier said than done in the 12th century), eating "natural" foods, wearing natural fibers, and living free of addiction and poor habits. Hildegard also believes that healing emerges as a direct result of compassion—a stunningly accurate reflection of Reiki principles—and that we can only help others through compassionate "ear diagnosis" (a medieval equivalent of "authentic listening"') which means listening "with the entirety of your heart"[1]—a truly beautiful concept.

Authentic compassion doesn't need an excuse to thrive, doesn't work around a calendar, and comes from the truest part of our hearts and spirit. What would our lives look like, how drastically would our behaviors and inclinations change, if we listened daily with our hearts? If we took more care with our hard-hearted words? Can you imagine?

A friend recently told me a story… Her son had come home from school with a little girl's headband that had snapped in two when someone had pushed her down. Wanting to console her, my friend's son told her that "his daddy could fix anything."

Despite his daddy's best efforts, the headband wasn't salvageable. Instead of sending his son to school to return the broken headband with regrets, or reinforcing the sad lesson that "life's not always fair," this man, exhausted from his shift work, still made the supreme effort; he went to the mall, hunted down the same headband in an unlikely shopping spree in a girls' accessory store, and delivered it to his son's classroom, and to the little girl, who couldn't stop smiling.

This man didn't give millions to a charity, write an act of legislation, end Middle Eastern strife, or fix climate change—he showed beautiful, selfless, loving compassion in a small but remarkable way. Perhaps most precious of all, he modeled for his son what humanity and compassion look like when offered from the heart in his family's little corner of the world. Consider what it might mean to choose compassionate, deliberate acts of kindness like this for ourselves and those we encounter daily. How would this change our stories? Compassionate lessons abound, if only we're willing to listen and learn.

I watch Züs, our outrageously gregarious tuxedo kitty, jump up and dislodge Nommie, the sweet-tempered, tiny tabby from the more preferable of two window perches. Züs plunks down and, in moments, is leaning back at a precarious angle with eyes closed as Nommie gently and carefully washes Züs' black and white throat. What a moment of selfless engagement, pure enjoyment, and unconditional love. Surely if animals can figure this out so can we…

As Buddha once said, "If you want to protect your feet from rocks and thorns, don't try to cover the whole word with leather, cover your own feet with shoes."[2] So few of us consciously examine and question whether our ingrained habits and patterns

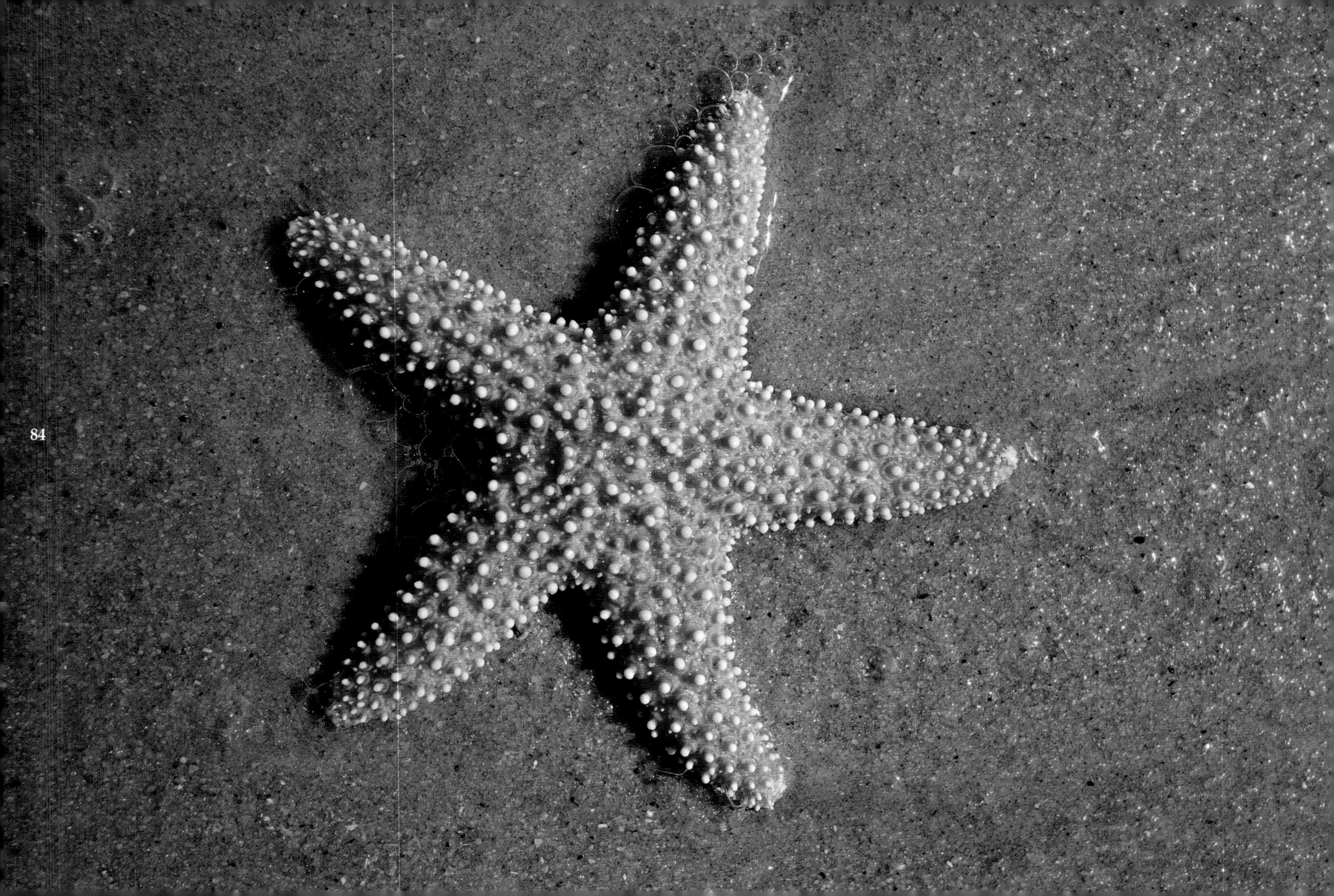

bring us the life and satisfaction we crave. Often we continue unconsciously, doing what we've always done, what our parents did, what's expected. On those rare occasions when we break free and open the door to change, evolution, and transformation, the Universe gifts us with new ways of being and seeing in the world. Change comes inevitably anyway, despite our best refusals, so why not own the transformation?

Just like forgiveness, before we can extend compassion and authentic caring love to another, we must first be willing and able to choose this for ourselves. Much in the way deliberate intent in our thoughts can wake up our potential and give rise to new hope, changing the stories we believe and tell about our histories, experiences, and essential selves can change the way we offer ourselves up to the world, allowing us to share compassion and give the most profound parts of us back to ourselves. Because every emotion and every thought is a current of energy, our potential is limitless; we can reinvent ourselves as many times as necessary to become someone who lives a positive, hopeful, open-hearted story.

Even before experts began studying bullying behavior, long ago as a youngster I already knew that razor-sharp cruelty comes from pain and sadness. Although I don't know what my father felt when he said or did terrifically painful things to my mother and me—or even *why* he did these things—I have learned that sometimes we are asked to open our hearts in unlikely ways. And so I have. I could continue to tell myself he hated me because I was unlovable, unworthy, a waste of space, but I'm not convinced those stories hold sway anymore; his motivation no longer matters because *my* story has finally shifted.

The energy keeping this pain alive—the same energy that keeps any pain alive—*belongs to me*. We are always already in charge of our choices, feelings, and our stories. How we modify these stories, how much we believe about our unlovable selves, dictates how able we find ourselves to gift others with our compassion and love.

The choice—how to be, how to act, how to love, how to transform—is ours, *always*. May you transform in peace and with an open heart.

Namaste.

Gentle compassion can be ours, to give and receive, but only with open, self-loving hearts. You've told yourself stories of lack many times— how you aren't quite smart, attractive, wealthy, or good enough. How you just don't match up. The time to transform, rally, and rewrite your devastating story is upon you. The time to feel your power has arrived.

Set Your Intention

Sit quietly with eyes closed. Breathe slowly in and out, until you settle on a comfortable rhythm. Consider with openness and honesty the places and spaces you dislike in your life. Do people respect you? Does your job fulfill you? Do your kids, spouse, or partner really and truly listen to you? If the answer to any of these is "no," what is the story you tell yourself about that person, job, or situation? Do you know for certain this story is true? Breathe slowly and set your intention using positive language:

I create truth.

I feel able to transform.

I am compassion.

Stating your intention in the positive is another way of respecting your higher self and creating a more kind, less harmful, more loving self-story.

Breathe the Reiki Energy

Find a quiet place and sit comfortably. Close your eyes and breathe deeply. Keeping your hands comfortably on your lap, make a loose fist with one hand and hold the opposing index finger inside the fist lightly. If lots of mental chatter fills your head, acknowledge it and then let it go. Envision a bright violet above your head, like a soft, peaceful cloud. With each in and out breath, allow the soft halo of color to come down and surround you like a shawl, enveloping your head, shoulders, chest, right down to your feet. It brings with it an amazing, fresh, clean, bright, invigorating energy. The light heals and transforms. Say the following with me:

All the power of the universe is here with me now.

You are transformation.

Acknowledge Your Message

You see yourself walking peacefully across a beautiful beach. Your arms swing freely at your sides and your mind and heart feel clear of worry. The sand feels pleasant and soothing on your feet as the sun warms your shoulders and back. You near the gentle wash of the tideline and notice ocean foam churning and boiling into a soft white froth far beyond the jetty. These impressive, crashing waves make quite a spectacle, but you stand quietly in the soft lap of the tideline, safe and protected.

Beautiful hunks of sandstone form the massive jetties just ahead of you, the result of millions of years' worth of collision and movement. Within the brown and gold-striped crevices, small basins create small, shallow pools where water trickles slowly in and out, leaving the rush of the waves behind. You step into one these knee-deep crystal clear pools, and gasp at the delicious warmth of the water.

At first you notice a plump red starfish lounging against a sediment rock. The rock's many stripes and layers create a beautiful contrast against the ruby-red animal. Then you notice with wonder how you are sharing this peaceful tidal pool with hundreds of starfish of all shapes, sizes, and colors. Some recline, some cling to rocks at awkward angles, and some swish slowly in the tidal basin's gentle sway. The pinks, grays, browns, and reds make a cacophony of color as starfish arms radiate at all degrees, making it difficult to know where one starfish begins and another ends.

You feel at total peace watching these silent animals rest and rejuvenate. Close your eyes in this moment of extreme peace. Breathe deeply. Hear the message they radiate to you with unconditional love, peace, and compassion.

Your ability to transform lies within this message. What do you see? Hear? Smell or taste? What do they want you to know?

However you experience this message, understand it speaks to your needs alone because you are so precious. Stand slowly, thanking the tidal pool and all its teeming life for the information that will help you to transform your life. Come back to the present and sit comfortably. Give silent thanks to the ocean and its animals.

In the same way a starfish can regenerate its arms, you too can regenerate your limiting beliefs about yourself. What message did the starfish have for you? Was it hard to hear? Hopeful? Difficult to digest? Write down this message in a private place. Even if the idea of rewriting your most essential story — the story by which you have identified yourself for many years — seems challenging or even impossible, today you will begin to give yourself love and compassion.

Take a moment to think about your life, and on a piece of paper make two columns. On the left, list at least ten limiting beliefs about yourself and their consequences. These can be large or small, seemingly insignificant or life changing. For example, if you can't cook well this belief could read, "I am a terrible cook, and so I/my family never has a satisfying meal." If you feel that your marriage or partnership is in danger, this belief might read, "My marriage is crumbling because I am a bad spouse/partner."

Write down a contrasting belief opposite the first item. It doesn't matter whether this seems like a stretch or impossibility, an unlikelihood or a fantasy of good feeling, write it down anyway. If you need to, refer back to your message, the gift that tells you how important you are to the world. After you have done this, if you feel inclined, journal for a few moments about what the new "story" behind this belief might look and feel like, how it would feel to be less judgmental about yourself.

Each day, reread the new belief from the day before, then move to the next limiting belief in the column and rewrite it in a positive, hopeful, open-hearted way. Remember to keep reading your message for inspiration and hope.

After you have rewritten limiting beliefs for the entire list, use the new, positive beliefs as affirmations you read to yourself or say aloud when you get up, at lunchtime, before you go to sleep, and anytime in between. Doing this simple

Stars & Stripes

Starfish have fascinated me since childhood. I remember paging through a reference book in our den, one full of unrecognizable genus and species in Latin accompanied by full color pictures. The Latin escaped me but the pictures did their job. The reds, the browns, tans, and purples were amazing and woke me up to all the watery possibilities of life beyond my sweet goldfish. Not only can starfish regrow missing limbs, but some can regenerate completely from a fragment, even when they've been torn apart. Unless you live in a tropical locale, you likely won't see starfish very regularly or easily, but I still love knowing they're down there somewhere, regenerating, regrowing, and literally rewriting the story of their little damaged starfish bodies in the most profound of ways. We would all be wise to heed the starfish's lesson: others may do what they will and say what they think, but I'll still be just fine—it's my right, my power, my story.

act—reading, reminding yourself, and reinforcing the new positive stories about your life—will work to empower and transform you. It really works!

No one except you can *make* you believe something you don't want to accept. Attacking, berating, chastising, and criticizing yourself takes you farther and farther from your divine purpose, from an open and compassionate heart, from God. What do you want to believe about yourself today? *This power is yours.*

Starfish Affirmation

I return to my own heart,   *tending the place within where compassion flows.*

Love and understanding blossom there.   *I release all but that which serves me.*

Resources

I offer the following resources as supplements to your natural healing practice. Since innate healing goes beyond the superficial, I have included titles and resources related to compassionate living, self-growth, crystal healing, and more. As always, follow your intuition and you will gravitate towards exactly what you need!

Chakra Healing

New Chakra Healing; Cyndi Dale

Color and Crystals: A Journey Through the Chakras; Joy Gardner

Your Aura & Chakras: The Owner's Manual; Karla McLaren

The Chakra Workshop: A Step by Step Guide to Regaining Your Body's Vital Energies; Anna Voigt

Motivational

The Success Principles: How to Get from Where You Are to Where You Want to Be; Jack Canfield

The Dark Side of the Light Chasers: Reclaiming your Powers, Creativity, Brilliance, and Dreams; Debbie Ford

Mutant Message Down Under; Marlo Morgan

Angelic Healing

Healing with the Angels; Doreen Virtue

Angel Medicine; Doreen Virtue

Earth Angels; Doreen Virtue

Metaphysical

Ask and It Is Given; Esther and Jerry Hicks

The Amazing Power of Deliberate Intent: Living the Art of Allowing; Esther and Jerry Hicks

Earth, Water, Fire, & Air: Essential Ways of Connecting to Spirit; Cait Johnson

Sea Magic: Connecting with the Ocean's Energy; Sandra Kynes

On Becoming an Alchemist: A Guide for the Modern Magician; Catherine MacCoun

Sacred Contracts: Awakening Your Divine Potential; Caroline Myss

Shamanic Reiki; Llyn Roberts

Shapeshifting: Techniques for Global and Personal Transformation; John Perkins

The Laws of Manifestation; David Spangler

Hildegard of Bingen's Spiritual Remedies; Dr. Wighard Strehlow

Aromatherapy

Daily Aromatherapy: Transforming the Seasons of Your Life with Essential Oils; Joni Keim & Ruah Bull

Aromatherapy & Subtle Energy Techniques; Joni Keim Loughran and Ruah Bull

The Fragrant Mind: Aromatherapy for Personality, Mind, Mood, and Emotion; Valerie Ann Worwood

Compassionate Living

The Joy Diet; Martha Beck

Finding Your Own North Star; Martha Beck

Radical Acceptance : Embracing Your Life with the Heart of a Buddha; Tara Brach

The Answer is Simple; Sonia Choquette

Letting Go of the Person You Used to Be: Lessons on Change, Loss, and Spiritual Transformation; Lama Surya Das

I Am Grateful: Recipes & Lifestyle of Café Gratitude; Terces Engelhart with Orchid

The Wise Heart: A Guide to the Universal Teachings of Buddhist Psychology; Jack Kornfield

The Craggy Hole in my Heart and the Cat Who Fixed It; Geneen Roth

Radical Forgiveness; Colin Tipping

The Sunflower: On the Possibilities and Limits of Forgiveness; Simon Wiesenthal

Jim Donovan, former Rusted Root drummer and transformational workshop facilitator: http://www.jimdonovandrums.com/

Crystal Healing

Laying on of Stones; D.J. Conway

Cunningham's Encyclopedia of Crystals, Gem & Metal Magic; Scott Cunningham

Crystal Wisdom; Dolfyn

The Crystal Bible: A Definitive Guide to Crystals; Judy Hall

Crystal Enlightenment; Katrina Raphaell

Crystal Therapy: How to Heal and Empower Your Life with Crystal Energy; Doreen Virtue, Ph.D. and Judith Lukomski

As always, FOLLOW your intuition...

Endnotes

Denying Fear

1. Das, Lama Surya. *Letting Go of the Person You Used To Be*. New York: NY, Broadway Books, 2003.
2. Beck, Martha. *Finding Your Own North Star*. New York: NY, Three Rivers Press, 2001.
3. Das, 138.
4. Andrews, Lynn V. *Jaguar Woman*. San Francisco, CA: Harper & Row Publishers, 1986.
5. Weschcke, Carl Llewellyn. "Listen! Listen to the Voices!" *New Worlds of Body, Mind & Spirit* catalog, March/April 2009.
6. "Magical Words; The Power of Affirmations," Karen Elizabeth Holbrook, accessed August 7, 2010, http://bayoudreamer.com/pdfs/Magical_Words.pdf.
7. Kynes, Sandra. *Sea Magic*. Woodbury: Maine, Llewellyn Publications, 2008.

The Movement of Forgiveness

1. Beck, Martha. *Leaving the Saints: How I Lost the Mormons and Found my Faith*. New York: NY, Crown Publishers, 2005.
2. Tipping, Colin. *Radical Forgiveness*. Boulder: Colorado, Sounds True, 2009.
3. Angelou, Maya and Jeffrey M. Elliot. *Conversations with Maya Angelou*. Jackson: Mississippi, University Press of Mississippi, 1989.
4. Ricaud, Matthew. *The Sunflower: On the possibilities and limits of forgiveness*, ed. Simon Wiesenthal. New York: NY, Schocken Books, 2009.

Dignifying Grief

1. Chopra, Deepak. *Ageless Body, Timeless Mind*. New York: NY, Harmony Books, 1994.
2. Kullander, James. "Here & There." The Omega Institute Newsletter, 2008.
3. Roth, Geneen. *The Craggy Hole in My Heart and the Cat Who Fixed It*. New York: NY, Harmony Books, 2004.

Touching Faith

1. "Saul David Alinsky." STANDS4 LLC, accessed November 23, 2010, http://www.quotes.net/quote/9996.

Alchemizing Hope

1. Canfield, Jack. *The Success Principles*. New York: NY, Harper, 2005.
2. Strehlow, Wighard. *Hildegard of Bingen's Spiritual Remedies*. Rochester: NY, Healing Arts Press, 2002.

Accepting Surrender

1. Matousek, Mark. *The When You're Falling, Dive: Lessons in the Art of Living*. New York: NY, Bloomsbury USA, 2009.

2. Beck, Martha. *Leaving the Saints: How I Lost the Mormons and Found my Faith*. New York: NY, Crown Publishers, 2005.

3. Kornfield, Jack. *The Wise Heart: A Guide to the Universal Teachings of Buddhist Psychology*. New York: NY, Bantam Dell, 2008.

Cultivating Compassion

1. Strehlow, Wighard. *Hildegard of Bingen's Spiritual Remedies*. Rochester: NY, Healing Arts Press, 2002.

2. Das, Lama Surya. *Letting Go of the Person You Used To Be*. New York: NY, Broadway Books, 2003.